# Model, Rig, Animate!

## with 3ds max 6

by Michele Bousquet

**Many Worlds Productions**
WWW.CLICK3DS.COM

## NOTICE TO THE READER

### Trademarks

Autodesk, Discreet, and 3ds max are registered trademarks of Autodesk, Inc.

### Contributors

Models on CD designed by Oscar Blanco
Models on CD created by John Paul Casiello and Michael McCarthy
Cover design and illustration by Michele Bousquet

Printed in the United States

For more information, contact:

Many Worlds Productions
30C Main St.
Raymond, NH 03077
(603) 895-3571
(603) 895-8434 fax
or visit our website at www.click3ds.com.

Questions or difficulties with publication or CD, email order@click3ds.com

# PREFACE

This book focuses on the basics of modeling, rigging, and animating low-poly characters with 3ds max, a complete modeling, animation and rendering software package by Discreet for Windows PC's.

In recent years, 3ds max has become the mainstay modeling program for numerous game development, broadcast, and film companies. Artists at these companies use many of the techniques described in this book to create their animated scenes.

The need for this book became apparent to me during day-to-day work with new animators attempting to learn how to model and rig their own characters. There are a few free resources on the Internet that can show you how to make a specific model, plus a couple of books that cover the topics from A to Z, but I couldn't find a simple, to-the-point resource that taught the basics for creating a model and rig while paving a foundation for more complex work.

Modeling and rigging are crafts that can take months or years to master, but they can also be used by the novice to start creating simple, rewarding scenes. Animating one's own visions is perhaps the most inspiring part of working in 3D, and I am of the opinion that you can start right here, right now. There's no need to learn every tool in 3ds max before you get results.

This book focuses on the fundamental techniques, going step-by-step with each tool so you know how it should be used. By the time you're done with this book, you'll be able to model, rig, and animate simple characters of your own design, and you'll be in great shape to take advantage of more complex techniques presented in other resources, such as the texts listed at the end of this book.

With this book, you're just a few steps away from making your visions a reality. May the learning process be enjoyable for you, and may you become the animator you've always dreamed of being.

*Michele Bousquet*

## HOW TO USE THIS BOOK

This book provides an introduction to low-poly character modeling, rigging, and animation with 3ds max.

The book is divided into four chapters:

*Chapter 1 - Character Modeling*: Model a low-polygon character.

*Chapter 2 - Character Rigging*: Create bones and a fully functional rig for the character.

*Chapter 3 - Skinning*: Apply the Skin modifier to the character and adjust its settings so the character mesh can be deformed by bones.

*Chapter 4 - Character Animation*: Use traditional principles of animation with 3ds max's tools to create finished animation.

The book is designed so you can go through it from beginning to end to create a complete project. Alternately, you can skip to sections that interest you. Numerous files are included on the CD that allow you to jump in just about anywhere and do the project.

The sections in each chapter consist of:

• An explanation of the tools needed for the next task,

• Optional *Practice Exercises*, and

• *Tutorials* for the project.

Practice exercises are named with single alphabetical letters (A, B, C, etc.) that continue throughout the book. Tutorials are named with a letter to signify the chapter, followed by a number. For example, the tutorials in the *Character Modeling* chapter are M1, M2, etc. In the *Skinning* chapter, they are S1, S2, etc.

If you want to skip the explanations and practice exercises and get right to the instructions, look for the Tutorials. If you want to use the techniques for your own project, read the explanation, do the Practice Exercises, and use the techniques for your own model.

## SUPPORT

If you have questions about this book or the accompanying CD, please email us for assistance at mra6@maxhelp.com.

## ABOUT THE CD

The CD that comes with this book contains files used in practice exercises and tutorials. When you need to load a file, you are given the filename as well as the folder.

On the CD you will find a number of *snapshot* files. These are files saved along the way during tutorials. When you are instructed to save a file with a particular filename, you will find a matching file on the CD. Feel free to load these files at any time to study them or check your work.

The CD contains the following folders:

*Animation* holds folders used in *Chapter 4, Character Animation*. It includes a *Scenes* folder with snapshot files, and an *AVI* folder with animation. Some of the AVI files are versions of animation created in this book; others are included just for fun.

*Characters* holds a selection of characters that you can use for rigging if you don't plan to model your own.

*Models* holds the files for *Chapter 1, Character Modeling*.

*Practice* holds practice scenes that you will load for practice exercises throughout the book.

*Rigs* contains files for *Chapter 2, Character Rigging* and *Chapter 3, Skinning*.

It is not necessary to copy files from the CD to your hard disk, but you can do so if you want to.

## FOR INSTRUCTORS

Lesson plans are available for use with this book. Email mra6@maxhelp.com if you would like to receive a copy of the lesson plans. We provide lesson plans free of charge to instructors.

## ACKNOWLEDGMENTS

Thank you to Oscar Blanco, John Paul Casiello and Michael McCarthy for their work on the characters on the CD, and an extra thanks for Michael for technical editing and advice on content. A thank you to Jason Gardino for providing the teenager stress-test.

A big thanks to Paul Neale for taking the time to show me his approach to rigging, and thus providing the foundation for the techniques in this book. Thanks also to Michael Comet for additional rigging tips.

Thanks to Precision Wordage, Inc. for proofing and other assistance.

And the biggest thank-you of all to my ever-patient husband David. A writer never had it so good.

# TABLE OF CONTENTS

# 1
# CHARACTER MODELING

The first step in the character animation process
is the creation of a character suitable for animation.

In this book, you will model, rig, and animate a simple character similar to the one shown at right. In this chapter, you will model the character.

To prepare for modeling, create two folders on your hard disk to save your scenes as you go along. Create a *Practice* folder to hold the practice exercises you do in preparation for the real thing, and create a *Models* folder to hold the models you create for the project.

## DEFINITIONS AND TERMS

These terms are used in this chapter when describing the modeling process. These terms are also found frequently in the 3ds max documentation.

*Model* - A three-dimensional (3D) representation created in a software package such as 3ds max.

*Face* - A flat, triangular area of a model. Models are made up of faces, and each face is surrounded by three lines called *edges*.

*Polygon* - A flat area of a model, usually rectangular, made up of two or more faces. A polygon is surrounded by edges, usually four but sometimes more. We'll be working mostly with polygons in this book.

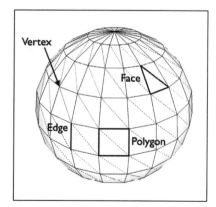

*Vertex* - A point where two edges meet. The plural for vertex is *vertices*.

*Low-poly* - A model is considered *low-poly* when it has relatively few polygons, which also means few faces and vertices. Low-poly models are often used in game development.

*Box modeling* - A modeling technique that starts with a primitive object such as a box or sphere. You can model just about anything with box modeling, including characters of any kind.

## REFERENCE PICTURES

Before starting to model, you should have reference drawings or photos of the character you want to make. Taking the time to sketch out the character, even roughly, will save you hours of modeling time.

Some modelers find it useful to scan in one or two reference pictures and display them right in the 3ds max viewports when modeling. There are two ways you can go about this:

- Set up one or two planes and map the pictures onto them, or

- Display each reference picture as a background in a viewport.

In this book we will use the first method, using the picture shown here as a guide to the proportions for our character.

---

### Practice A: DISPLAYING THE REFERENCE PICTURE ON A PLANE IN THE SCENE

1. Choose *File menu* > *Reset* to reset 3ds max.

2. In the Front viewport, create a **Plane** object of any size. You can find the **Plane** creation command in the same place you find the **Box** and **Sphere** commands, on the default **Create** panel.

   A plane is similar to a box, but it has no thickness. A plane is ideal for placing reference images in a scene.

3. Press the **[M]** key to open the Material Editor.

4. In the Shader Basic Parameters rollout, check the **2-Sided** option.

   This will make the picture show up on both sides of the plane.

5. In the Blinn Basic Parameters rollout, under Self-Illumination, change the **Color** value to **100**.

   This will make the picture show up in the scene regardless of the amount or direction of the lighting.

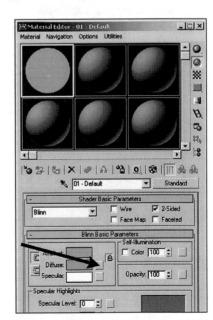

6. In the Blinn Basic Parameters rollout, click the small box next to the **Diffuse** color swatch, and choose **Bitmap** from the Material/Map Browser. Select the file you want to use as a background. You can use any picture for practice.

---

7. Select the plane, and click **Assign Material to Selection** on the Material Editor.

8. Turn on the **Show Map in Viewport** option on the Material Editor.

   The picture appears on the plane in the Perspective viewport. You can make it appear in other viewports by right-clicking the viewport label and choosing *Smooth+Highlights* from the pop-up menu.

   If the reference image doesn't appear to have the correct proportions, you'll need to change the plane's length and width.

## Practice B: DISPLAYING A REFERENCE PICTURE AS A BACKGROUND

You won't use this method of displaying reference images in this book, but it's useful to know how to do it. You might find you prefer this method for your own scenes.

1. Load 3ds max.

2. Activate the viewport in which you want the reference picture to appear.

3. Choose *Views menu > Viewport Background* to display the Viewport Background dialog.

4. Click **Files**, and choose the reference picture from the file selector dialog that appears. You can practice with any picture you like.

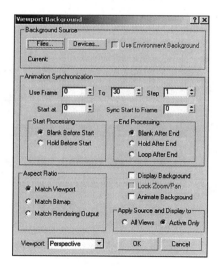

5. On the Viewport Background dialog, make sure the **Display Background** checkbox is checked.

6. Set Aspect Ratio to **Match Bitmap**, and check the **Lock Zoom/Pan** checkbox.

   When **Lock Zoom/Pan** is checked, the picture will zoom when you zoom the viewport. If you don't check this option, the picture won't zoom in or out along with your model, and it will be difficult to use the reference picture effectively.

7. Click **OK** to display the picture in the current viewport. Zoom in or out of the viewport to see the entire picture.

Here, you'll display the reference picture *SkaterFront.jpg* as a background in the Front viewport so you can use it as a guide when modeling.

## Set up the Material

1. Locate the file *SkaterFront.jpg* in the *Models/Maps* folder on the CD. Copy this file to the *3dsmax6\Maps* folder on your hard disk.

2. In 3ds max, create a **Plane** in the Front viewport. Set its parameters as follows:

| | |
|---|---|
| **Length** | 410 |
| **Height** | 380 |
| **Length Segs** | 1 |
| **Width Segs** | 1 |

3. Press the **[M]** key to open the Material Editor.

4. In the Shader Basic Parameters rollout, check the **2-Sided** option.

5. In the Blinn Basic Parameters rollout, under Self-Illumination, change the **Color** value to **100**.

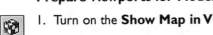

6. In the Blinn Basic Parameters rollout, click the small box next to the **Diffuse** color swatch, and choose **Bitmap** from the Material/Map Browser. Select the file *SkaterFront.jpg*.

7. Click **Assign Material to Selection** on the Material Editor.

## Prepare Viewports for Modeling

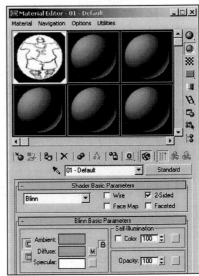

1. Turn on the **Show Map in Viewport** option on the Material Editor.

2. Right-click the Front viewport label, and choose *Smooth&Highlights* from the pop-up menu.

   This causes the image to be visible in the Front viewport, where you will do most of your work.

3. Click **Zoom Extents All**, located at the lower right of the screen to show the plane in all viewports.

4. Right-click the Perspective viewport label and choose *Texture Correction* from the pop-up menu.

   Turning on *Texture Correction* causes the system to use a small amount of extra resources to display the bitmap correctly.

5. To turn off the grid display in each viewport, activate each viewport and press the **[G]** key on the keyboard. This makes the reference picture easier to see.

6. Right-click the Front viewport label and choose *Edged Faces*. Do the same for the Perspective viewport.

   This will enable you to see the edges on the box after you create it.

## START WITH A BOX

Most low-poly models start with a box primitive. As you gain experience with box modeling, you might find that a sphere or cone works better for some of your characters. In this book we focus on a human-type character, which is easier to create from a box than a cylinder or sphere.

You'll smooth the box later, so very few polygons are needed at the start.

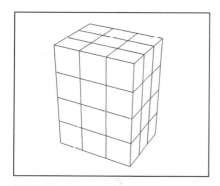

### Tutorial M2: CREATING THE INITIAL BOX

1. In the Top viewport, create a Box primitive. Set its parameters as follows:

   | | |
   |---|---|
   | **Length** | 70 |
   | **Width** | 90 |
   | **Height** | 125 |
   | **Length Segs** | 3 |
   | **Width Segs** | 3 |
   | **Height Segs** | 4 |

2. In the Top viewport, move the box downward so it sits in front of the plane.

3. In the Front viewport, move the box so the top of it aligns with the skater's shoulders in the reference picture.

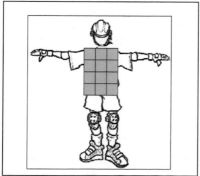

## CONVERTING THE BOX

Before beginning the box modeling process, you'll convert the box to an Editable Poly or Editable Mesh. The conversion won't change the shape of the box, but it will change the way the box can be edited. You'll need these editing tools to create the character.

When a box is created, you can go to the Modify panel and change its Height, Length and Width parameters. When you convert a box to an Editable Poly or Editable Mesh, you can no longer access these parameters. They will be replaced by other tools that you can use to push and pull the box into shape.

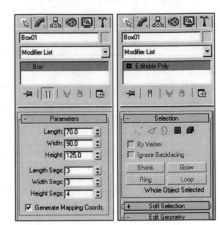

An Editable Poly has slightly different tools than an Editable Mesh. For 95% of box modeling tasks, the tools are the same for both types of objects, but there are a few situations where the unique Editable Poly tools come in handy. You'll see the reason for using Editable Poly more clearly later on, when we get down to smoothing and modeling details.

---

## Tutorial M3: CONVERTING THE BOX TO AN EDITABLE POLY

Now you will convert your character's box to an **Editable Poly**.

1. With the box selected, go to the **Modify** panel.

   This displays the *modifier stack*. The modifier stack currently has only one listing: **Box**.

2. Right-click the **Box** listing in the modifier stack, and choose *Editable Poly* from the pop-up menu.

   The box is converted to an Editable Poly, and the original box parameters are no longer accessible.

3. Change the name of the object to **Body**.

4. Save the scene in your *Models* folder with the filename **LPChar01.max**.

   The letters in the filename stand for **Low Poly Char**acter.

---

## SHAPING WITH POLYGONS

Once the primitive is converted to an Editable Poly, the first step is to form limbs off the main box. You'll do this by pulling out existing polygons to create new ones, then shaping the new polygons. This process is called *extruding*.

Before you can manipulate polygons, you must access the Polygon sub-object level.

<table>
<tr><td>

**☝ TIP ☝**

*It's a good practice to save your work often as you model the character. In the tutorials, you will be instructed when to save, but you can save as often as you like.*

</td></tr>
</table>

### ACCESSING AND SELECTING POLYGONS

You can access the Polygon sub-object level in either of two ways:

- Click the [+] next to the Editable Poly listing on the modifier stack and choose Polygon from the list that appears, or

- Click the Polygon button on the Selection rollout.

Now you can select the polygons you wish to manipulate. Click any polygon, and you will see the edges around it turn red to indicate that the polygon is selected.

You can select polygons in the same ways you select objects:

- Hold down [Ctrl] and click to select additional polygons.

- Hold down [Alt] and click to unselect polygons.

- Draw a selection region around polygons to select or deselect several at once.

To make the selected polygons appear as solid red, you can turn on the *Shade Selected Faces Toggle*. Press [F2] to turn this feature on and off.

## Practice C: SELECTING POLYGONS

Here, you will practice accessing the **Polygon** sub-object level and selecting polygons.

1. Before working on your scene, save the file as **PracticeC.max** in your *Practice* folder.

   This will prevent you from accidentally saving over your project file.

2. Hide the reference plane to make it easier to work with the box. To do this, select the plane with the reference picture, then right-click and choose *Hide Selection* from the Quad menu.

3. Change the Perspective view to a User view. To do this, activate the Perspective viewport and press the **[U]** key on the keyboard.

4. Press the **[F2]** key on the keyboard to turn on the *Shade Selected Faces Toggle*.

5. On the **Modify** panel, access the **Polygon** sub-object level.

6. Select any polygons the box.

   The polygons will turn a bright, solid red to indicate that they are selected. If they don't, press **[F2]** again to toggle the display.

7. In the User viewport, use **Arc Rotate** to rotate the view. Hold down the **[Ctrl]** key and click on polygons on another side of the box.

8. Continue selecting polygons until you can do it easily on any part of the box.

   Keep this file on your screen for use in the next practice exercise.

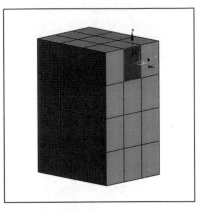

---

☙ **TIP** ☙

*Use Arc Rotate only in the User viewport. Using it another viewport will turn that viewport into an angled User view. You don't need more than one User view onscreen at a time, and you need to retain your Top, Front and Left views for accurate modeling..*

*If you accidentally turn a Top, Front or Left viewport into a User viewport, press [T], {F] or [L] on the keyboard to change the viewport back to its original display.*

---

☙ **TIP** ☙

*If Arc Rotate causes the object to rotate out of view, try using Arc Rotate Selected instead. To do this, click and hold the Arc Rotate button until a flyout with three buttons appears. Choose the middle button, where the circle at the center of Arc Rotate is solid white.*

*Now, when you rotate the view, the object will stay centered in the viewport.*

---

## EXTRUDING POLYGONS

With box modeling, you form limbs by pulling new polygons out from the original box. The process of pulling new faces out from an object is called *extruding*.

 Locate the Extrude parameter on the Edit Polygons rollout. Click the Settings box next to the extrude parameter to display the Extrude Polygons dialog.

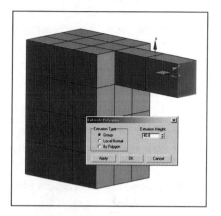

Change the Extrusion Height, and watch the viewport to see if you like the change. If so, click Apply to set the change.

After you click Apply, the Extrusion Height will be permanently added to the selected polygons, then a further extrusion with the same parameters will be displayed in viewports. This new extrusion won't be applied permanently until you click Apply or OK.

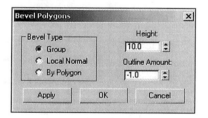

If you don't want to extrude the selected polygons any more, you can click Cancel to set the previously applied changes, or OK to set the currently displayed change in addition to previously applied changes. You can also select other polygons while this dialog is open and apply changes to them.

You can extrude and scale polygons at the same time by using the Bevel command. This command extrudes with the Height parameter, and scales the end of the extrusion with the Outline Amount. You can use a negative value as the Outline Amount to reduce the size of the extrusion end.

Here, you'll practice using these tools on your box. In the tutorial that follows, you'll reload the saved file and create the arms for real on your character project.

### Extrude Polygons

1. Select the box you used in the last practice exercise. Go to the **Modify** panel, access the **Polygon** sub-object level, and select some polygons.

2. On the Edit Polygons rollout, click the **Settings** button next to **Extrude**. The Extrude Polygons dialog appears, and the **Extrusion Height** is temporarily applied to the selected polygons.

3. Change the **Extrusion Height** parameter, and press **[Enter]** so you can see the temporary result.

4. Click **Apply**.

   The extrusion is permanently applied to the polygons, and a new extrusion is displayed on the selected polygons.

5. In any viewport, select a different set of polygons. As you select the polygons, note that the **Extrusion Height** is temporarily applied to them.

6. Continue to experiment with the **Extrude** tool until you understand how it works. When you have finished, click **OK** to set the changes and close the dialog.

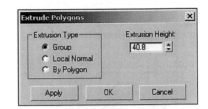

### Bevel Polygons

1. Select a polygon that hasn't been extruded.

2. Click the **Settings** button next to **Bevel**. The Bevel Polygons dialog appears.

3. Change the **Height** to **20** and the **Outline Amount** to **-8** to cause the selected polygons to both extrude and scale.

4. Click **Apply**.

   At this point, the last extruded polygons might look rather pinched. The parameters you just applied to the originally selected polygons have been temporarily applied again, and this extreme scaling causes them to pinch.

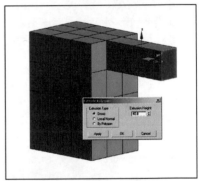

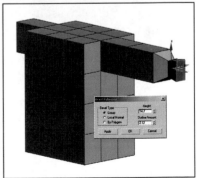

5. Change **Outline Amount** to a positive number, causing the ends of the polygons to widen out. Click **Apply**.

6. Continue to experiment with the Bevel tool until you feel comfortable using it. When you have finished, click **OK** to exit the dialog and set the changes.

## Tutorial M4: CREATING THE ARMS

Now you're ready to apply what you've learned about polygons to your project. Here, you'll select two polygons on the box, one on each side, then you'll extrude them to form the character's arms.

### Prepare the Scene

1. Load the file *LpChar01.max* that you created earlier. If asked if you want to save the current scene, click **No**.

   It's a good idea to freeze the reference plane so you don't select it by accident while modeling the character. Before you freeze it, you'll need to tell 3ds max not to turn it gray upon freezing.

2. Select the reference plane. Right-click the viewport and choose *Properties* from the Quad menu.

3. In the Display Properties group of the Object Properties dialog, turn off the **Show Frozen in Gray** checkbox. Click **OK** to close the dialog.

4. Right-click the viewport, and choose *Freeze Selection* from the Quad menu.

   The reference plane is still visible, but you can't select it. If you need to select it in the future, just right-click any viewport and choose *Unfreeze All*.

5. Change the Perspective view to a User view by activating the Perspective viewport and pressing the **[U]** key on the keyboard.

6. Press the **[F2]** key on the keyboard to display selected polygons in red.

### Select Arm Polygons

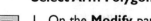

1. On the **Modify** panel, access the **Polygon** sub-object level. Select the top center polygon on one side of the box. The polygon will turn a bright, solid red to indicate that it's selected.

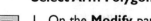

2. In the User viewport, use **Arc Rotate** to rotate the box around to the other side. Hold down the **[Ctrl]** key and click on the corresponding polygon on the other side.

   One polygon on each side of the box is now selected. Next, you will extrude these polygons to make the arms.

**☀ TIP ☀**

*You can open a recently-used file by choosing File menu > Open Recent.*

## Extrude the Arms

We'll use the **Bevel** tool to extrude the arms since this tool offers the fastest workflow. We won't try to shape the clothing just yet -- first we'll work on roughly shaping the body, then later we'll shape the clothing and other details.

1. Click the **Settings** button next to **Bevel**. The Bevel Polygons dialog appears.

2. Set **Height** to **40** and **Outline Amount** to **-7**. Click **Apply**.

   Don't be concerned that the extruded arms don't match exactly with the reference picture. We're using the picture as a guide for size, not necessarily for an exact match.

3. Enter these values on the Bevel Polygons dialog, and click **Apply** after you enter each set.

| Body Part | Height | Outline Amount |
|-----------|--------|----------------|
| Elbow | 16 | 2 |
| Lower Arm | 45 | -5 |
| Base of Hand | 9 | 5 |
| Palm of Hand | 15 | -1 |

Now you'll extrude the neck. You'll create the head separately later, so you'll create only a neck extrusion for the head to sit on.

4. In the User viewport, select the neck polygon at top center of the box, where the head will protrude from the body.

5. If you closed the Bevel Polygons dialog, open it again. Set **Height** to **30** and **Outline Amount** to **-4**. Click **OK** to apply this extrusion and close the dialog.

6. Save the scene as **LPChar02.max**.

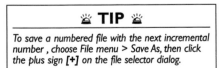

---
### ☼ TIP ☼
---
*To save a numbered file with the next incremental number , choose File menu > Save As, then click the plus sign [+] on the file selector dialog.*

## Tutorial M5: Extruding the Legs

Next, you will extrude and shape the legs. You'll use the **Bevel** tool again, but this time you'll use it interactively rather than typing in specific values. You can use this tool interactively by clicking the **Bevel** button itself, dragging on selected polygons in a viewport to extrude them, then moving the cursor again to scale the end polygon.

 1. In the User viewport, use **Arc Rotate Selected** to rotate the view so you can clearly see the bottom of the box.

2. Arrange the Front viewport so you can see the character's legs.

3. Select the two polygons on the bottom that are directly below the arms. Refer to the picture to make sure you're selecting the right ones.

4. Click the **Bevel** button. Be sure to click the button that actually says **Bevel**, and not the **Settings** button you clicked earlier.

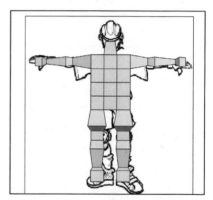

5. While watching the Front viewport, click and drag one of the selected polygons in the User viewport. until the two extrusions reach the tops of the character's shorts. Release the cursor, and move the mouse to flare the shorts slightly. Click to set the extrusion.

6. Click and drag again on the end polygons, and extrude to the tops of the knees. Release the cursor and scale the end polygons down to fit the knees. Click to set the extrusion.

7. Continue extruding polygons to create the legs. When you reach the feet, simply extrude an ankle and a stump for now. You will extrude the actual feet later on.

Don't worry if your model doesn't look exactly like the one shown here. Box modeling takes practice! If you don't like the result, reload **LPChar02.max** and try again.

8. When you're satisfied with the model, turn off the **Bevel** button and save your work as **LPChar03.max**.

## SHAPING WITH VERTICES

Extruding and outlining polygons will get you only so far in box modeling. At some point, you'll have to start moving vertices around to get the model into shape.

 To work with vertices, you must first access the Vertex sub-object level. To do this, you can choose Vertex from the modifier stack, or click the Vertex button on the Selection rollout. Then you can start selecting vertices and moving them around.

Characters are usually more round than boxy, so the first thing you'll want to do is smooth out the sharp corners. Then you can start shaping the body, arms and legs to more closely match the reference picture.

To shape your model, work on one part at a time, such as the shoulders, chest, hips or arms.

Select vertices as best you can in one viewport, then use other viewports to add or subtract from the selection. Move and scale vertices as necessary.

Always check more than one viewport to ensure you have the correct vertices selected before moving or scaling.

---

### ☀ TIP ☀

*For the best results, use any viewport to select vertices, but use the Top, Front and Left viewports to move vertices, not the User or Perspective viewport.*

*If you move vertices in the User or Perspective viewports, you can easily move vertices to unwanted places, then wonder why your model is crumpled or mangled.*

---

## Tutorial M6: Shaping the Body with Vertices

1. In the Top viewport, use a selection region to select the vertices at the four outside corners of the box.

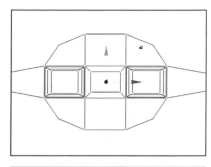

2. Scale the selected vertices inward on the XY plane to make the character body rounder.

3. Select the vertices at the top and bottom of the neck protrusion, and move them upward to create a shoulder area.

4. Select the vertices between the tops of the thighs (on the underside of the box), and move them downward to create a hip area.

5. Select the vertices around each arm where the arm meets the shoulder, and scale these vertices away from the arm to smooth the transition from the body to the arms.

6. Work with the vertices on the model until it looks similar to the pictures shown.

7. Save the scene as **LPChar04.max**.

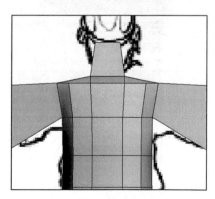

## SMOOTHING TOOLS

The beauty of low-poly modeling is that you can work with a very simple model, yet smooth it out quickly and effectively when necessary. Smoothing is great for checking the model's shape or rendering the scene. When you're actively modeling or animating the character, you can turn the smoothing off to make your work much faster and easier.

Now that the box is starting to resemble a character, we can smooth it out and see how it's shaping up.

### NURMS SUBDIVISION

One of the features of an Editable Poly is that you can smooth it without adding any modifiers. This can be accomplished with the Editable Poly's NURMS subdivision feature.

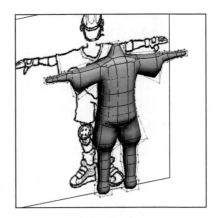

This is a very effective way to work with a model that is nearing completion. You can work with the low-poly model itself while still seeing what the finished model will look like.

### Practice E: USING NURMS SUBDIVISION

 1. Go to the base level of the **Editable Poly** object. You can do this by clicking **Editable Poly** on the modifier stack, or by turning off the **Vertex** button on the Selection rollout.

2. On the Subdivision Surface rollout, check the **Use NURMS Subdivision** checkbox. By default, **Iterations** in the Display Group is set to 1. If you want it to look even smoother, change **Iterations** to **2**.

 3. Now access the **Vertex** sub-object level. You can see the vertex "cage" that defines the shape of the model. When you move vertices, the smoothed model also changes.

We won't be using this method here, so let's turn it off.

4. Return to the base level of the **Editable Poly** object, and uncheck **Use NURMS Subdivision** to turn it off.

**☃ TIP ☃**

*It might be tempting to turn the Iterations setting up very high to make the character very smooth, but this will cause the system to perform very slowly. If your model needs more than 2 Iterations to smooth it, there is probably something wrong with the underlying structure, such as tangled vertices or polygons.*

## MESHSMOOTH

Another option for smoothing the model is the MeshSmooth modifier. The advantage of using the MeshSmooth modifier is that you can turn it off quickly by clicking the light bulb next to the modifier on the modifier stack. Compare with the NURMS Subdivision method, where you have to return to the base level of the Editable Poly object every time you want to turn off smoothing.

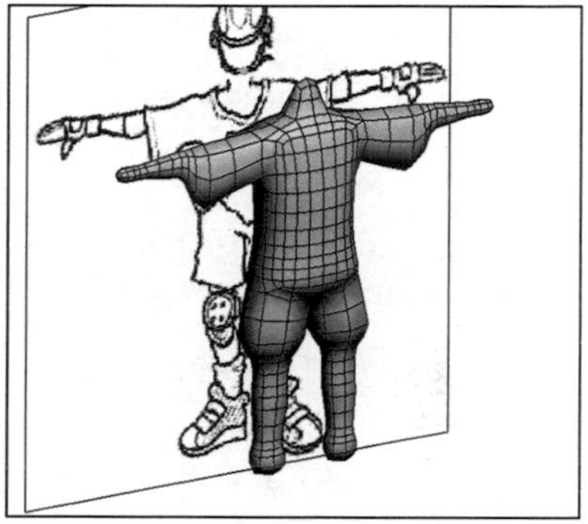

## Tutorial M7: Applying MeshSmooth to the Character

1. Apply the **MeshSmooth** modifier to the **Editable Poly** object.
2. In the Subdivision Amount rollout, set **Iterations** to **1** or **2**.

   This smooths out the model, but it doesn't appear to have any more polygons than it had before.
3. In the Local Control rollout, uncheck the **Isoline Display** checkbox.

   Turning off **Isoline Display** shows the edges for the actual polygons on the object. However, it's easier to work with this display turned off.
4. Check the **Isoline Display** checkbox to turn it back on.

   You can modify the object at the **Vertex** sub-object level while viewing the smoothed model, just as you can with the NURMS subdivision method.

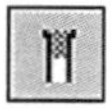

5. Turn on the **Show end result on/off toggle**.

   This will show the results of the smoothing no matter what level of the modifier stack is active.

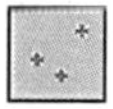

6. Access the **Vertex** sub-object level of the **Editable Poly** object.

   Be sure to access the **Vertex** sub-object level for the **Editable Poly** object, not the **MeshSmooth** modifier.
7. Click the light bulb next to the **MeshSmooth** modifier to turn it off for now. You'll turn it on again later to help you check your work.
8. Save your work as **LPChar05.max**.

**TIP**

*Isolines are lines that use the same number of edges to display the mesh, even when there are more polygons due to smoothing. When Isoline Display is turned on, you see only the original number of edges, not the actual number of edges in the smoothed mesh.*

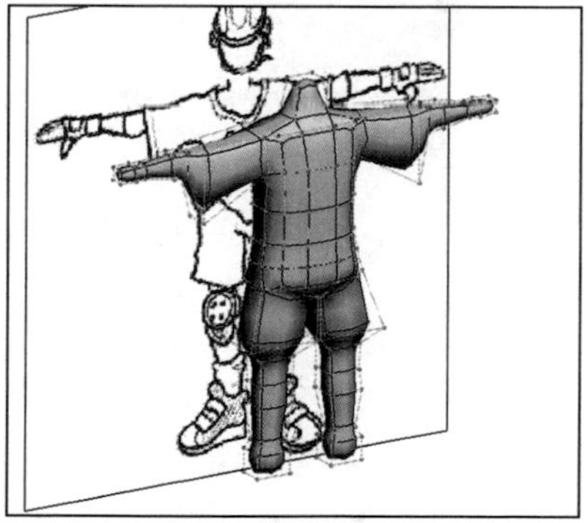

# THE SLICE TOOL

Currently, the areas where the clothing end and the body begins are not well-defined. This can't be solved simply by adjusting vertices, as there aren't enough vertices and edges to make the necessary detail.

This problem can be solved with the Slice tool. Slice cuts new edges in a polygon, creating new edges and vertices for you to manipulate.

## Practice F: Using the Slice Tool

1. Reset 3ds max.

2. Create a cylinder in the Top viewport. On the **Modify** panel, right-click the cylinder listing on the modifier stack, and choose *Convert to Editable Poly*.

3. Set the Front and Perspective viewports to display *Smooth+Highlights* and *Edged Faces*.

4. Access the **Polygon** sub-object level, and select the polygons at the center of the cylinder.

5. Click the **Slice Plane** button on the Edit Geometry rollout.

   A large yellow plane appears in the scene. This is the slice plane.

6. In the Front viewport, move and/or rotate the slice plane so it passes through the selected polygons in the place where you would like to cut the polygons.

   As you move the slice plane, you can see where the cut is going to take place by looking at the Perspective view. The location of the new edges changes as you move the slice plane.

7. When you're sure the slice plane cuts through the selected polygons, click the **Slice** button.

   New edges are cut where the slice plane passes through the selected polygons.

8. If you want to slice more polygons, move the slice plane and click **Slice** again.

9. When you're done slicing, be sure to turn the **Slice Plane** off.

   You can save this scene if you like, but it is not necessary.

## Tutorial M8: Slicing Detail on the Arms

Here you will use the **Slice** tool to cut extra detail on the arm to help shape the clothing. You will cut new polygons just below the elbow.

### Prepare to Slice

1. Load the file *LPChar05.max* that you created earlier.

2. In the Top viewport, zoom in on the left arm.

3. Select the character's body.

4. Access the **Polygon** sub-object level.

5. Select the polygons in the elbow area.

   To ensure you select the polygons on the front, sides, and back of the arm, use a selection region when selecting the polygons.

### Slice New Polygons

1. In the Edit Geometry rollout, click **Slice Plane**.

2. Move and rotate the slice plane so it passes through the selected arm polygons.

   When viewed in the Top viewport, the slice plane should appear as a single straight line.

3. Click **Slice**.

   New polygons have been cut at the lower arm.

4. Click **Slice Plane** to turn it off.

5. Select the same polygons on the opposite arm, and repeat the procedure to slice polygons on that arm.

6. Save your work with the filename **LPChar06.max**.

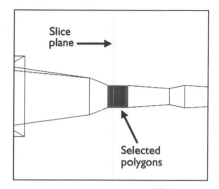

Slice plane →

Selected polygons

---

☀ **TIP** ☀

*To help you rotate the slice plane by exactly 90 degrees, turn on the the Angle Snap Toggle on the main toolbar. When this option is turned on, any object you rotate will turn in increments of 5 degrees.*

## SHAPING OVERHANGS

Now that you have more detail to work with, you can start to shape the overhanging parts of the clothing, such as the sleeves and pant legs. You do this by moving vertices near the clothing's openings inward past the sleeve or pant leg.

Ordinarily, you don't want to overlap vertices with their neighbors when box modeling. Shaping the overhangs is the exception. Perform this step carefully to avoid mangling your mesh.

### Tutorial M9: SHAPING THE SLEEVES

1. Access the **Vertex** sub-object level of the **Editable Poly** object.

   Be sure to access the **Vertex** sub-object level for the **Editable Poly** object, and not for the **MeshSmooth** modifier.

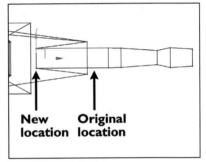

New          Original
location   location

2. Select the vertices at the elbow, the ones closest to the sleeve.

3. Move these vertices toward the torso and past the edge of the sleeve, as shown at right.

   Take care to move the vertices well past their neighbors, and not right on top of other vertices. If you move vertices on top of one another, they will be very hard to select later on.

4. Click the light bulb next to **MeshSmooth** to turn it back on.

5. On the modifier stack, click **Show end result on/off toggle** to turn it on, if it's not already on.

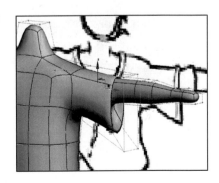

6. Check the look of the smoothed model. You might have to move the selected vertices farther inward to fully shape the sleeve.

7. Repeat this procedure on the other arm to make another sleeve.

8. Check the sleeves in the Front viewport. If necessary, move the vertices around the edge of the sleeves to match them to the reference picture more closely.

9. Save your work with the filename **LPChar07.max**.

## Tutorial M10: Shaping the Pant Legs

You'll use the same method you used on the sleeves to form the pant legs. You can perform this procedure with **MeshSmooth** turned on or off.

1. If necessary, use the **Slice Plane** and **Slice** command to cut new edges just below the knee. You can select both legs at once, and slice the new edges on both legs at the same time.

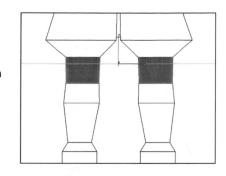

2. Move the original knee vertices up inside the pant leg to form the cloth overhang.

   Be sure to turn on **MeshSmooth** to check that vertices have been moved far enough to form the overhang.

3. Check the model against the reference picture in the Front viewport. Move vertices as necessary to match the shorts in the reference picture.

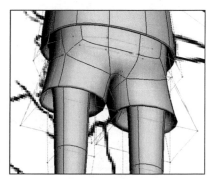

4. Slice another set of edges around around the area where the shirt meets the shorts.

5. Scale the new vertices to make a baggy shirt bottom, and move vertices to make the shirt overhang.

6. Save your work with the filename **LPChar08.max**.

---

☀ **TIP** ☀

*It is often easier to add detail than remove it, so it's best to start with fewer polygons and use Slice to add them as needed.*

# THE HAND

The next step is to add fingers to the hand. Rather than the four fingers on a regular human hand, we'll create a three-fingered hand with a thumb. This is a very common hand setup for cartoon-style characters. Mickey Mouse, for example, has only three fingers in addition to his thumb.

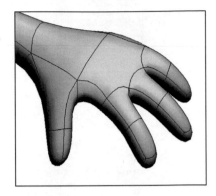

In shaping the hand, we'll work with just the left hand, then later on we'll mirror the hand over to the right side.

## Tutorial M11: CREATING THE THUMB

You will use **Bevel** to extrude the thumb from the hand.

 1. Access the **Polygon** sub-object level.

2. Select the thumb polygon on the left hand.

 3. Click the **Settings** button next to **Bevel**.

4. On the Bevel Polygons dialog, set **Height** to **7**, and **Outline Amount** to **-2**. Click **Apply**.

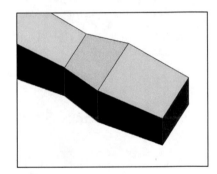

5. Set **Outline Amount** to **-1.5**.

6. Click **OK** to set the change and close the dialog.

 7. Access the **Vertex** sub-object level. In the Top viewport, shape the thumb vertices individually to resemble the picture.

8. Save your work with the filename **LPChar09.max**.

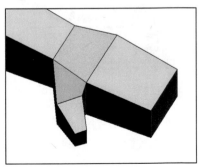

# Tutorial M12: Slicing Polygons for the Fingers

The palm is not wide enough to accommodate three fingers, but you can easily fix that by scaling the polygon. However, there is another problem: You currently have only one polygon to extrude for the fingers. You need three fingers, so you'll have to use the **Slice** tool again to make more polygons for finger extrusions.

This is yet another task where the **Slice** tool comes in handy. The **Slice** tool is excellent for creating the extra polygons needed for fingers, toes and other protrusions.

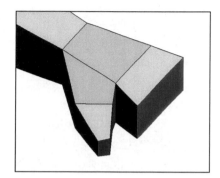

1. Using either the **Vertex** or **Polygon** sub-object level, shape the left hand with moving or scaling until it looks similar to the picture above right.

2. Select the polygon at the end of the hand.

3. Right-click the Left viewport label, and choose *Views > Right* from the menu.

   The viewport now shows the right side of the character rather than the left. Now you can clearly see the selected polygon in the Right viewport.

4. Click **Slice Plane**.

5. Rotate and move the slice plane so it cuts through the end of the hand about 1/3 of the way over from the left end when viewed in the Right viewport.

6. Click **Slice**.

7. Move the slice plane so it is about 2/3 of the way over from the left end of the hand. Click **Slice**.

8. Click **Slice Plane** to turn it off.

   You now have three polygons at the end of the hand.

9. Save your work as **LPChar10.max**.

## EXTRUDING MULTIPLE POLYGONS

We have our multiple finger polygons, and we're just about ready to extrude. Before doing this, we'll move the center finger vertices outward a little. This will cause the fingers to extrude outward from one another at an angle, making the fingers easier to select individually after they're extruded.

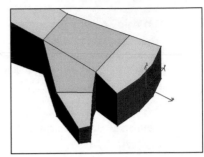

Now we're ready to extrude. You figure all you have to do is access the Polygon sub-object level, select the end finger polygons, extrude them, and... Oh, no! The fingers extrude as one mass rather than as three individual fingers. Not a pretty sight.

Never fear, the Editable Poly is here. Remember when I said it had some advantages over an Editable Mesh object? One feature is that it can extrude multiple polygons separately rather than as one mass. We'll use this feature to extrude the fingers.

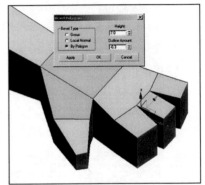

### Tutorial M13: EXTRUDING THE FINGERS

 1. Use the **Vertex** sub-object level to move the center hand vertices outward a little and prepare for finger extrusion.

 2. Access the **Polygon** sub-object level. Select the three finger polygons on the left hand only.

 3. Open the **Bevel** Polygons dialog by clicking the **Bevel Settings** button. Select **By Polygon** as the **Bevel Type**.

   Turning on **By Polygon** will cause the polygons to extrude separately.

4. Change the **Height** value to **7** to make the first extrusion, and set **Outline Amount** to **-0.3**. Click **Apply**.

5. Set **Outline Amount** to **-1.2**. Click **OK** to apply this setting and close the dialog.

 6. Turn on the **MeshSmooth** modifier to see how the fingers look. Go to the **Vertex** sub-object level. Adjust the finger vertices as necessary to curl the fingers slightly and make a nice-looking hand.

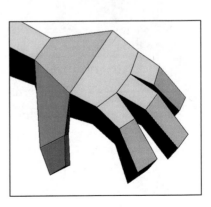

7. Save your work with the filename **LPChar11.max**.

## DETACHING AND ATTACHING MESH PARTS

Earlier, I mentioned that you should work with one hand only for the time being, as we would copy and paste the finished hand to the other side. To do this, you'll use the Detach tool to detach the geometry as a separate object, then use Attach to attach it to the other side.

## Tutorial M14: COPYING AND PASTING THE HAND

### Detach and Copy the Left Hand

1. Turn off the **MeshSmooth** modifier if it's still turned on.

2. Access the **Polygon** sub-object level, and select all the polygons that make up the left hand.

3. On the Edit Geometry rollout, click **Detach**.

4. On the Detach dialog, check **Detach as Clone**. Enter the name **Right Hand** as the object name, and click **OK**.

### Mirror the Detached Hand

1. Return to the **Editable Poly** level of the object. Otherwise, you won't be able to select the new Right Hand object.

2. Select the **Right Hand** object.

3. Make sure the Front viewport is active.

4. On the Main Toolbar, click **Mirror Selected Objects**. On the Mirror Screen Coordinates dialog, make sure the **X** axis is selected, and click **OK**.

   The hand is mirrored around the center of the body, so the hand will always land in correct place exactly on the other side of the body. If the hand doesn't align with the wrist, this means the wrist on the original body object should be adjusted, not the hand. You will deal with this in later steps.

### Delete the Original Hand Polygons

There are a few polygons on the right side of the body that make up the stub of the right hand. You will delete these polygons so you can attach the new hand to the body.

1. Select the body, and access the **Polygon** sub-object level.

2. Select the polygons that make up the stub of the right hand attached to the body.

3. Press **[Delete]** on the keyboard. When asked if you want to delete isolated vertices, answer **Yes**.

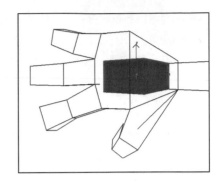

### Weld the Wrist

Next, you will attach the new right hand to the body, and weld the wrist.

1. Access the **Vertex** sub-object level.

2. Move the wrist vertices at the end of the arm to align with the hand's wrist vertices. Move them first in the Top viewport, then line them up in the Front viewport.

Now you'll attach the two objects together.

3. On the Edit Geometry rollout, click **Attach**, then click the new right hand.

The hand is now part of the same object as the body. This will allow you to weld the vertices together at the wrist.

4. Click **Attach** to turn it off.

5. Select all the vertices at the wrist.

6. Click the **Settings** button next to Weld.

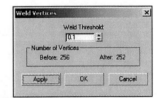

The Weld Vertices dialog appears. Under Number of Vertices, the **After** value should be exactly 4 less than the **Before** value, which indicates that by welding, you are going to reduce the 8 vertices in the wrist area (4 on the hand and 4 at the wrist) to 4 vertices.

If the **After** value isn't 4 less than the **Before** value, increase the **Weld Threshold** value, until it is so. Alternatively, you can try moving vertices at the wrist closer to their corresponding vertices.

7. Click **Apply** to weld the vertices, then click **OK** to close the dialog.

If all has gone well, the hands on both sides of the body now match.

8. Save your work with the filename **LPChar12.max**.

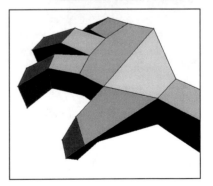

With what you know now, you can shape the shoes, socks and additional details. The fronts of the shoes can be created with a simple extrusion from the front of the foot. The socks and hi-top sneakers can be shaped by slicing some new edges and moving them up over neighboring edges, as you did with the shirt and pants.

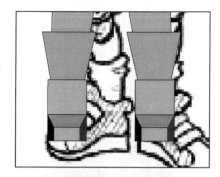

## Shape the Socks and Shoes

1. Extrude the polygons at the fronts of the feet to form the shoes.

2. Use the **Slice** tool to slice new edges near the knees.

3. Scale the new vertices so they are wider than the rest of the leg. Pull the wide vertices up past the adjacent vertices to form the socks.

4. Use the **Slice** tool to slice new edges near the ankles. Scale the new vertices to be wider than the rest of the ankle.

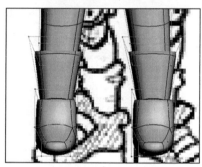

5. Move the vertices up to form the tops of the hi-top sneakers.

## Shape the Stomach and Shoulders

1. Shape the character's belly by moving the stomach and shirt vertices toward the center of his body in the Right viewport.

2. The shoulders are also a bit boxy. Move the points between the armpits and chest downward and inward to round out the chest.

3. Check the model carefully to see if any other parts need adjustment. Use what you've learned to adjust the model for smoothness.

4. Save your work as **LPChar13.max**.

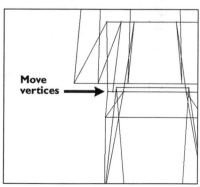

Move vertices →

# CREATING NEW EDGES

Our character is looking pretty good. Congratulations on getting this far! The only obvious thing lacking is a shirt collar. In order to make this shape, you're going to learn some advanced box modeling techniques.

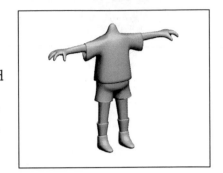

To add the sleeve and pants detail, you sliced existing polygons and moved the vertices around. You could do the same to cut new edges for the shirt collar, but this would take a long time. Instead, you're going to create new edges in the shape of the shirt collar. To add an edge, you need vertices to set the beginning and end of the edge, so you'll need more vertices.

You can create more vertices by dividing existing edges, then connecting the vertices to make new edges.

## Tutorial M16: SHAPING THE COLLAR

Here, you'll divide edges around the collar to create new vertices, and create new edges from the vertices. The **Divide** tool is available only for Editable Mesh objects, so you must convert the mesh to an Editable Mesh first.

### Convert to Editable Mesh

1. In the Right viewport, move the model farther away from the reference plane. This will enable you to reach the back of the model when dividing edges.

2. Remove the **MeshSmooth** modifier by highlighting it and clicking **Remove modifier from the stack**.

3. On the **Modify** panel, right click the **Editable Poly** listing and choose *Convert to Editable Mesh*.

4. On the **Display** panel, turn on the **Vertex Ticks** checkbox.

   This will enable you to see the new vertices as they are created.

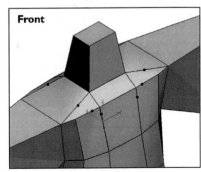

Front

5. Use **Arc Rotate Selected** to rotate the User or Perspective view until you have a clear view of the model's shoulder area.

### Divide Edges

1. Access the **Edge** sub-object level. On the Edit Geometry rollout, click **Divide**.

2. In the User view, click the edges around the collar area to create vertices in a t-shirt collar pattern. Use the picture at right as a guide to where to click.

3. Rotate the view with **Arc Rotate Selected** so you can work with the back of the model. The vertices that are already at the back will be sufficient, so you only need to add vertices in the back shoulder area.

4. When you have finished, click **Divide** to turn it off.

5. Access the **Vertex** sub-object level. In the Front viewport, line up the vertices so they form a smooth collar shape.

6. Convert the mesh back to an Editable Poly.

## Set up Snaps

To create new edges to form the collar, you'll need to set up snap tools.

1. Locate the **Snap Toggle** button on the Main Toolbar. If the button doesn't display the number **3**, click and hold the button to choose the button with the **3** on it from the flyout. This selects the **3D Snap Toggle**.

2. Right-click the **3D Snap Toggle**. The Grid and Snap Settings dialog appears.

3. On the Grid and Snap Settings dialog, uncheck all selections, and check **Vertex**. Close the dialog by clicking the **[X]** at its upper right corner.

4. Click the **3D Snap Toggle** button to turn it on, if it isn't already on.

## Create New Edges

1. On the Edit Geometry rollout, click **Create**.

2. Move the cursor over one of the new vertices and watch for the snap cursor, small blue cross. When the snap cursor appears around the vertex, click to start the edge. Then move the cursor to the other vertex that will form the edge, and click. An edge is formed between the two vertices you just clicked.

3. Continue clicking on pairs of vertices to create edges and shape of the shirt collar. Use **Arc Rotate** to rotate the view if necessary.

4. When you have finished, turn off the **Create** button, turn off the **Vertex Ticks** display, and turn off the **3D Snap Toggle**.

5. Check the collar edges in all viewports, and make adjustments as necessary.

6. Save your work as **LPChar14.max**.

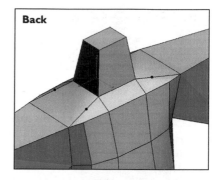

Back

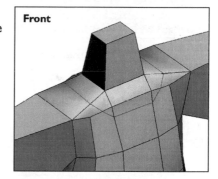

Front

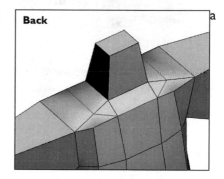

Back

## CHAMFER AND COLLAPSE

Now that you have edges to define the collar, you'll need an extra set of edges to pull inward and form the collar rim. This can be accomplished with the Chamfer tool. Chamfer makes two edges from one, splitting the two edges apart from the original location.

After performing a Chamfer, you might find that you need to clean up the model a little bit. Sometimes Chamfer leaves very small polygons, much smaller than the others around it, which can cause problems later on. You can fix these polygons by fusing two of the vertices around the polygon together with the Collapse tool.

### Tutorial M17: Creating the Collar Rim

#### Chamfer the Collar Edge

1. Access the **Edge** sub-object level.

2. Select the edges that form the collar, all around the front and back. The selection should form a continuous line all the way around the collar.

3. Click the **Settings** button next to **Chamfer** on the Edit Edges rollout.

4. Increase the **Chamfer Amount** to about **2** to create the two edges, and click **OK**.

#### Clean up the Polygons

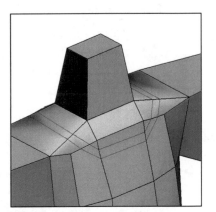

There is a little problem with the back of the collar. The chamfering process left two very small polygons at the back. Because these polygons are so small in comparison to the others around them, they will cause problems when you reapply **MeshSmooth**.

The **Collapse** tool fuses two vertices together, so you can use it to fix this problem. You can fuse two of the three vertices around the polygon together to change the triangle into a single edge.

1. Rotate the User view so you can see the back of the model.

2. Locate the two small faces formed by the collar rim.

3. Access the **Vertex** sub-object level.

4. Select the two vertices at the bottom of the triangular polygon.

5. On the Edit Geometry rollout, click **Collapse**.

   The two vertices are fused together, and the polygon is closed up.

6. Repeat this operation on the other polygon's vertices to close it up.

7. Save your work with the filename **LPChar15.max**.

### Form the Collar Rim

Here you will move the outer collar vertices to form the collar rim.

This is the tricky part. So far you've worked with edges and vertices that are relatively easy to see, select, and move. You'll need to learn a new technique for selecting and moving vertices to do this next step.

To properly form the collar rim, you'll need to rotate the User view with **Arc Rotate** to find and select vertices, then move the vertices in the Front or Left viewports. This process is sometimes tedious, and there may be times when you wonder if you'll ever understand what you're looking at. But it's important that you try this technique and get the hang of it in order to move on to more advanced tools.

1. Access the **Vertex** sub-object level.

2. Use **Arc Rotate** to find the vertices that form the outer edge of the collar. Select each of the vertices.

3. Move the vertices upward, and scale them inward to fold over the collar.

   You'll need to adjust the vertices manually to make the fold sit right. Eventually, you want the collar rim to look uniform, as shown in the picture.

4. In the Front viewport, locate an area that doesn't look right. Rotate the User view until you figure out where the errant vertices are, and select them right away in the User or Perspective view while you still know where they are. Then move the vertices in the Front or Left viewport.

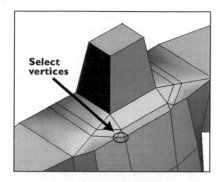

Select vertices

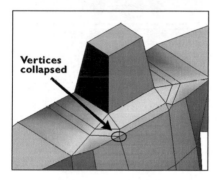

Vertices collapsed

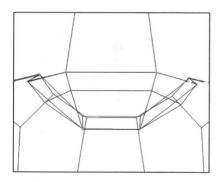

That last step will take some practice. The trick is to think only about finding vertices when rotating the User or Perspective view. Once you've found the vertices, select them quickly without looking away from the User or Perspective viewport -- otherwise you'll forget where they are! Then, when working in the Front or Left viewports, think only about moving the vertices.

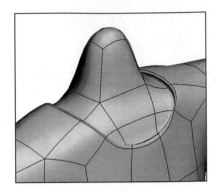

By switching between these two sets of views, you can find and move any set of vertices. That's the whole trick. Learn it well, as you'll need it when you do more complex modeling.

5. Check your work by reapplying the **MeshSmooth** modifier with **Iterations** of **1** or **2** and looking at the collar rim. It should be smooth and uniform all the way around.

6. Save your work with the filename **LPChar16.max**.

   This completes the modeling for the body. If you plan to animate the character, you might want to slice more edges at the knees and elbows to give the character more of an ability to bend his legs and arms. I'll leave that decision to you.

## THE SYMMETRY MODIFIER

In this book, you were instructed to build both sides of the character from scratch. However, you could have created one half and mirrored it to the other side with the Symmetry modifier.

Modeling with the Symmetry modifier has two advantages:

- You only have to model one half of the figure.

- The model is guaranteed to be symmetrical, which saves time during the rigging process.

This book instructed you to create both sides manually because you learned more tools that way, tools you'll need for more complex character modeling. In addition, when you're new to character modeling, it can be hard to visualize the entire character when you're working with only half of it.

If you want to try out the Symmetry modifier, you can do so, but it's not necessary for finishing this particular character.

1. Load the latest version of the character model, and remove the **MeshSmooth** modifier from the body model.

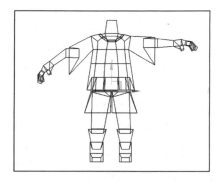

2. Access the **Vertex** sub-object level. Alter some part of the model so you can see the effect of the **Symmetry** modifier in later steps. For example, you might move one of the arms up or down.

3. Exit the **Vertex** sub-object level.

4. Apply the **Symmetry** modifier to the body.

5. Access the **Mirror** sub-object level of the **Symmetry** modifier. To do this, click the **[+]** next to the Symmetry modifier and highlight the **Mirror** listing that appears.

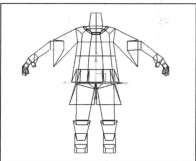

6. Move the **Mirror** sub-object around to see the effect on the character. You will need to turn on **Slice Along Seam**. You can also try different **Mirror Axis** settings, including **Flip**.

7. When the character looks the way you want it to, right-click the **Symmetry** modifier and choose *Collapse All* from the pop-up menu to turn the character into an **Editable Poly** again.

8. Reapply the **MeshSmooth** modifier.

9. Save the scene with *File menu > Save As* and **[+]**.

# THE MULTI/SUB-OBJECT MATERIAL

A Multi/Sub-Object material applies two or more materials to one object. This type of material is actually made of up several different sub-materials, each of which will be applied to different parts of the body.

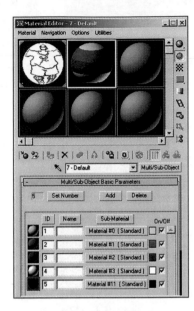

## Tutorial M18: MAKING A MATERIAL FOR THE BODY

### Create the Material

1. Press **[M]** to open the Material Editor.

2. Select an unused sample slot.

3. Click the button labeled **Standard**, and choose **Multi/Sub-Object** from the Material/Map Browser.

   When asked if you want to discard or keep the current material, choose to discard.

4. On the Material Editor, click **Set Number**, and set the number to **5**.

   Five materials are now displayed.

5. Click the color swatch at the far right of each material, and set colors as follows:

   | | |
   |---|---|
   | **Material 1** | **Fleshtone** |
   | **Material 2** | **Red** |
   | **Material 3** | **Blue** |
   | **Material 4** | **White** |
   | **Material 5** | **Black** |

   As you set the material colors, you will see different-colored stripes appear on the sphere in the sample slot.

### Set Material IDs

Now you need to tell 3ds max which parts of the body to apply each material to. This is accomplished with *material IDs*. By default, every polygon is assigned a material ID at the time the object is created. When you assign a Multi/Sub-Object material to an object, the material numbers correspond to the material IDs for the polygon.

Here, you'll set material IDs manually so different parts of the character correspond to the various materials..

1. Select the body and access the **Polygon** sub-object level. Select all the polygons in the body.

If you like, you can work with the **Show end result on/off toggle** turned on so you can see how the selection affects the smoothed mesh. If you do so, keep in mind that you will be selecting polygons displayed by the yellow cage, not the polygons on the mesh surface that were created by **MeshSmooth**.

2. In the Polygon Properties rollout, locate the **Set ID** value. Set this value to 1.

This resets all the material IDs to 1, giving you a clean slate to work with.

3. Select the polygons that form the character's shirt, and change **Set ID** to **2**.

4. Set material IDs for the remaining character parts as follows:

| | |
|---|---|
| **Pants** | 3 |
| **Socks** | 4 |
| **Shoes** | 5 |

5. In the modifier stack, go to the **Editable Poly** level for the body.

6. On the Material Editor, click **Assign Material to Selection**.

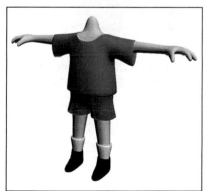

This applies the Multi/Sub-Object material to the body. The colors of the polygons on the body now correspond to the colors in the Multi/Sub-Object material, matched up by material ID. Check around the collar and pant legs to ensure you've set all the material IDs correctly.

The body model is now complete!

7. Save your work with the filename **LPChar17.max**.

## MODELING THE HEAD

Creating a low-poly head is a task that demands patience and practice. If you've ever tried to draw a realistic face or sculpt one from clay, you know that representing the human face is not a trivial task. Add to that the limitations of a low polygon count, and you can imagine the challenges that lie ahead.

In this section, I'll walk you through the steps for making a low-poly head that resembles an action figure or doll. Making a photorealistic head would take many more steps, but the same tools can be used.

When doing the tutorials in this section, don't be discouraged if your results don't come out quite as expected. Simply load the last file and try again.

Practice is the watchword here. Just as you wouldn't expect your first clay sculpting attempt to look perfect, so it is with low-poly facial modeling.

### REFERENCE MATERIALS

As with the character's body, you would do well to use reference materials when modeling a low-poly face. Action figures, toys and dolls are particularly good references for low-poly facial references as they do a great job of representing the human face without a lot of detail.

Personally, I have a collection of figures from favorite animated films such as *Toy Story* and *The Little Mermaid*, plus a few Warner Brothers characters. If you visit your local fast-food chain when they're running a film or cartoon promotion, you can gather up quite a number of figures for the meager cost of a burger and fries.

At right is a rendering of the low-poly head we'll create in this book. I used a combination of action figures to determine what the face would look like.

## THE SPHERIFY MODIFIER

You might think that facial modeling would start with a sphere. However, I've found that the arrangement of faces on a sphere is not the best for facial models. A box works much better. We'll apply the Spherify modifier to the box to form it into a spherical shape, then smooth the box's edges and mold the object into a head shape.

We'll create the face in a separate scene, then merge it into the body scene later on.

### Tutorial M19: Creating the Head

1. Reset 3ds max, saving any changes to the body that you have recently made.

2. In the Top viewport, create a box of any size.

3. Go to the **Modify** panel. Change the parameters to the following:

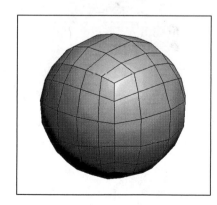

| | |
|---|---|
| **Length** | 70 |
| **Width** | 70 |
| **Height** | 70 |
| **Length Segs** | 4 |
| **Width Segs** | 6 |
| **Height Segs** | 5 |

Figuring out how many segments to put on a box for a low-poly model requires a bit of guesswork. I settled on this arrangement by trial and error.

4. Apply the **Spherify** modifier to the box.

The box is now shaped like a sphere.

5. Right click on the **Spherify** listing on the modifier stack and choose *Collapse All* from the list that appears. If a message appears asking to you confirm that you want to collapse, click **Yes**.

The model is collapsed to an **Editable Mesh**.

6. Right-click the **Editable Mesh** listing and choose *Convert to Editable Poly*.

Now you have a sphere-shaped box converted to an **Editable Poly**, and ready to be shaped into a head.

7. Save the scene as **LPHead01.max**.

## SMOOTHING GROUPS

You may have noticed something about this spherified box -- in a shaded view, you can clearly see the edges of the original box. This is due to something called *smoothing groups*.

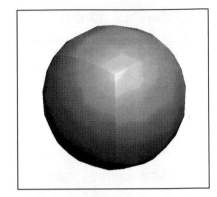

When an object is created, each face is assigned one or more smoothing group numbers. When the object is shaded or rendered, 3ds max compares each face's smoothing group number against the adjacent faces' numbers.

If the numbers on two adjacent faces match, 3ds max makes a smooth transition between the colors of the two faces, making the area appear round and smooth. If the numbers don't match, 3ds max makes no effort to smooth the color transition, and the edge between the two faces appears hard.

Smoothing group numbers are assigned automatically when an object is created. When a box is created, all the faces on one side of the box are assigned to smoothing group 1, the faces on the next side are assigned to smoothing group 2, etc. This causes each side of the box to appear smooth while the edges between sides appear hard and sharp. This is not desirable for a sphere, especially one to be used to model a face. You want the surface to appear smooth all the way across.

Smoothing groups can be changed at the Face or Polygon sub-object level of an Editable Mesh or Editable Poly. Changing smoothing groups affects only the way the model is shaded and rendered, not the model's shape.

Note that a face can belong to more than one smoothing group. In other words, each face can have more than one number associated with it.

### Smooth the Head Object

1. Access the **Polygon** sub-object level.

2. Select all polygons on the object by drawing a selection region around it.

3. On the Polygon Properties rollout, in the Smoothing Groups section, click the button labeled 1.

   All selected polygons are assigned to smoothing group 1, and the sphere appears smooth.

### Shape the Head

The first step in making a character's head is to shape the sphere into the rough shape of the head. This should be done before starting to model any of the character's facial features.

Imagine what your character's head would look like without eyes, nose or mouth. This is the type of shape we want to achieve with the sphere before continuing. The easiest way to do this is to shape the head at the **Vertex** sub-object level.

There are no special tricks for this task, just a little work and some patience.

1. Access the **Vertex** sub-object level.

2. Move, rotate and scale vertices until the head looks like an action figure head without eyes, nose or mouth. Use the pictures at right as a guide.

3. Save your work as **LPHead02.max**.

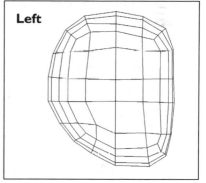

Left

### Prepare to Make the Facial Features

Most of your work will be focused on the front part of the sphere, where you'll mold and shape the eyes, nose and mouth. You won't need to work on the back of the head for some time.

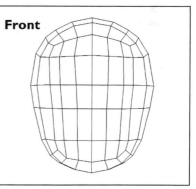

Front

Since you'll be selecting a lot of vertices, edges and polygons, and you don't want to accidentally select the back of the head when you want the front, your work can be made easier by hiding the polygons at the back of the head.

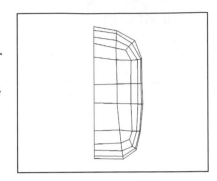

 1. Access the **Polygon** sub-object level.

2. In the Top or Left viewport, select all the polygons that make up the back half of the head.

3. On Edit Geometry rollout, click **Hide Selected**.

   The polygons at the back of the head are hidden, along with their vertices and edges. This will make them impossible to select by accident.

4. Save your work as **LPHead03.max**.

# CREATING FACIAL DETAILS

Okay, now comes the fun part. You'll start by making the face by defining areas for the eyes, nose, and mouth.

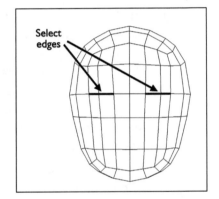

Select edges

In modeling the body, you learned that the Chamfer tool can be used to create two edges from one. You'll use this tool to make more edges for the facial features.

Since you know how to use Chamfer, I won't give you all the instructions in detail. You can either click Chamfer and do it that way, or use the Settings button next to Chamfer.

## Tutorial M21: DEFINING THE FACIAL FEATURES

 1. Access the **Edge** sub-object level.

2. Select the edges for the eyes, as shown in the picture.

3. Chamfer with an amount of about **4** to make the shapes for the eyes.

4. Select the edge for the nose, as shown in the picture.

5. Chamfer to about **3**.

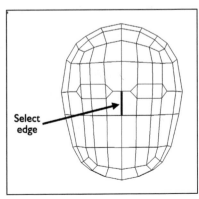

Select edge

6. Select four edges for the mouth, as shown in the picture.

7. Chamfer to about **3**.

8. Chamfer again to a little less than **3**, just large enough to form lips, but so the new lip chamfer lines don't overlap each other.

9. Save your work as **LPHead04.max**.

## EYE SOCKETS

You'll start by shaping the most recognizable feature of a humanoid face, the eyes. Eyes are more than just holes in the head. They have an almond shape, and are almost pinched at the corners.

First you'll adjust the vertices that form the eye shapes, and then you'll do a little extruding to form the eye socket and eyeball areas.

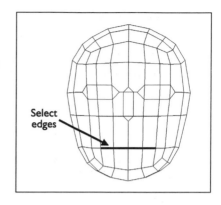

Select edges

## Tutorial M22: SHAPING THE EYE SOCKETS

### Make the Basic Eye Shape

1. Access the **Vertex** sub-object level.

2. Select the 2nd and 4th column of vertices on each eye, as shown at right.

3. In the Front viewport, scale the vertices vertically by about 50%.

4. Access the **Polygon** sub-object level.

5. Select all the polygons that make up the eyes.

6. Use **Bevel** to change the **Height** to **-3**, then set **Outline Amount** to **-1.5**.

7. Select the vertices at the centers of the eyes. In the Front viewport, scale these vertices vertically to about 200%.

8. Apply the **MeshSmooth** modifier to the head. Set **Iterations** to **1**.

   The eyes sockets are pinched at the corners, but they're starting to take shape.

9. Save your work as **LPHead05.max**.

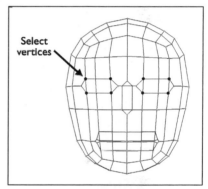

Select vertices

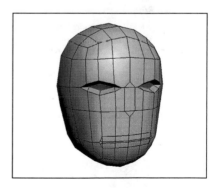

## Fix the Pinches

The pinching problem that has developed around the eyes is not unusual when box modeling, especially when you've created new edges with the **Chamfer** and **Bevel** tools. You can see the problem most markedly when you turn on **MeshSmooth** and turn off **Isoline Display**.

In general, pinching occurs when two or more vertices are too close to one another. The solution, fortunately, is simple. Chances are you only need one vertex at that spot, so you can simply collapse the vertices into one, and get fewer polygons in the bargain.

Finding the place where the vertices are close together is the trickiest part of this process. You'll have to find the vertices and select them before you lose track of them.

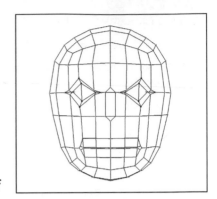

1. Turn off **MeshSmooth** if it's still turned on.

2. Access the **Vertex** sub-object level of the **Editable Poly**.

3. In the Front viewport, zoom in one of the eyes. Locate the places at each corner where three vertices are tightly grouped together.

4. Select one group of three vertices, and click the **Collapse** on the Edit Geometry rollout.

5. Select the other group of three vertices, and click **Collapse** again.

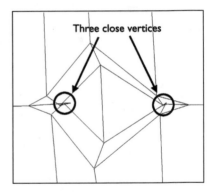

If want you to see the effect this has had on the eye pinching, turn on **MeshSmooth** and view the eyes in the Front viewport. Do you see the difference between the two eyes?
The collapsed side is much cleaner.

6. Turn off **MeshSmooth**.

7. Repeat the collapsing process on the other eye.

8. Check your work carefully to ensure you haven't collapsed too many vertices.

9. Save your work as **LPHead06.max**.

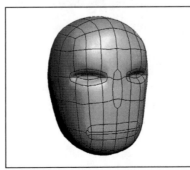

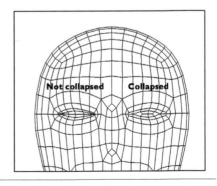

## NOSE DETAIL

We need more detail for the nose. We'll add the detail by adding vertices and connecting them to create more edges. Then we'll extrude the polygons to start making the nose. Once the nose is extruded, you'll collapse some of the vertices to remove unnecessary detail.

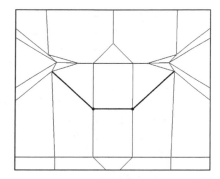

## Tutorial M23: Shaping the Nose

### Convert to Editable Mesh

1. Remove the **MeshSmooth** modifier from the stack.

2. Convert the head to an *Editable Mesh*.

   Now you can use the **Divide** tool to add more detail to the nose.

### Create New Edges

1. Access the **Edge** sub-object level.

2. Click **Divide**. Click at the center of each of the two longest nose edges to create two new vertices.

3. Turn on the **3D Snap Toggle**.

4. Click **Create** to turn it on.

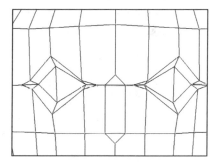

5. Click on each of the two nose vertices to connect them.

6. Click at the lower inside corner vertex of one eye, then click on the nearest new nose vertex to connect the two. Repeat for the other side of the nose.

7. Turn off the **3D Snap Toggle**.

### Bevel the Nose

1. Convert the head back to an *Editable Poly*.

2. Access the **Polygon** sub-object level. Select the three nose polygons.

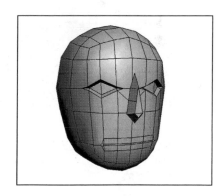

3. Use **Bevel** to increase **Height** to **2**, and **Outline Amount** to 1.

4. Increase **Height** to about **4**, and change **Outline Amount** to **-2**.

5. Save your work as **LPHead07.max**.

## Remove Detail

You currently have much more detail than you need to make the nose. Let's collapse some vertices and make things less complicated.

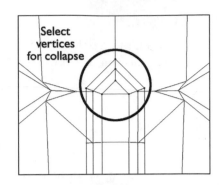
Select vertices for collapse

1. Access the **Vertex** sub-object level.

2. Select all the vertices at the top of the nose. Click **Collapse**.

3. In the User view, zoom into the middle part of the nose and rotate around until you can see the middle side vertices on one side of the nose. Select the two vertices as shown in the picture, and click **Collapse**. Repeat for the other side of the nose.

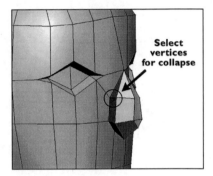
Select vertices for collapse

4. In the Left viewport, adjust vertices for a nice-looking profile.

5. Apply the **MeshSmooth** modifier and check your work. Make any further adjustments to the nose to make it look good. For example, you can scale the vertices at the tip of the nose horizontally in the Front viewport to make a wider nose.

6. Save your work as **LPHead08.max**.

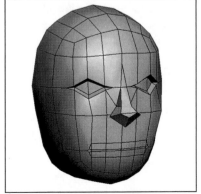

## THE MOUTH

After all your work on the eyes and nose, shaping the mouth is relatively simple. It's just more of the same, extruding and collapsing.

### Tutorial M24: Extruding the Lips

1. Turn off **MeshSmooth** if it's still turned on.

2. Access the **Polygon** sub-object level. Select the eight polygons that make up the lips.

3. Use **Extrude** to set **Extrusion Height** to **2** to extrude the lips.

4. Access the **Vertex** sub-object level. Select all the vertices at one corner of the mouth, including the vertices at the top and bottom of the lips. Click **Collapse**. Repeat for the other side of the mouth.

5. Turn on **MeshSmooth**, and make any necessary adjustments to the lips. For example, in the Front viewport, you can select all mouth vertices all the way across the head, and move them upward to move the mouth closer to the nose. You can also move the mouth vertices individually to shape the lips.

6. Save your work as **LPHead09.max**.

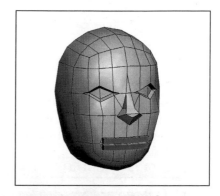

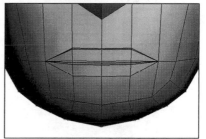

# FINISHING THE HEAD

The basic shape of the face is complete. Now you only need to tidy up the head and make fine adjustments to the shape of the head and face.

At the back of the head, there is nearly as much detail as there is at the front. This level of detail is not really necessary to define the basic round shape of the head, especially since most of it will be covered with hair. One easy way to reduce the number of polygons on the head is to collapse vertices at the back of the head.

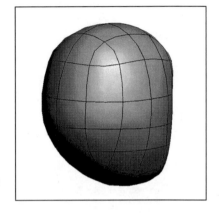

## Tutorial M25: REDUCING THE POLYGON COUNT ON THE HEAD

1. Turn off **MeshSmooth** if it's still turned on.

2. Access the **Polygon** sub-object level.

3. On the Edit Geometry rollout, click **Unhide All** on to unhide all polygons.

4. Access the **Vertex** sub-object level.

5. In the Selection rollout, turn on **Ignore Backfacing**.

   This will prevent you from selecting vertices on the side of the head opposite the one you're looking at.

6. Use **Arc Rotate** to look at the back of the head in the User viewport.

7. On the back of the head, select a pair of vertices to collapse. Click **Collapse**.

8. Continue to choose pairs of vertices, and collapse each pair once it has been selected. Take care when selecting vertices to ensure you don't select the wrong ones before collapsing.

   This process takes a while, but you will be rewarded with a much lower polygon count for the head.

   Make any other adjustments that you wish to the face and head. For example, you can move the eyes closer together, or shape the cheekbones and chin.

9. Save your work as **LPHead10.max**.

# CREATING FACIAL MATERIALS

In the same way you used a Multi/Sub-Object material for the body, you will also create and apply several materials for the face. You'll use a Gradient Ramp map to make the eye pupils.

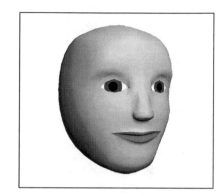

## Tutorial M26: Creating Materials for the Face

### Set Material IDs

1. Access the **Polygon** sub-object level.

2. Select all the polygons on the head. On the Polygon Properties rollout, change **Set ID** to 1.

3. Select the polygons that make up the whites and pupils of the eyes. There are two polygons for each eye. Set the ID to **2**.

4. Select the polygons that make up the lips. Set the ID to **3**.

### Set Colors for Skin and Mouth

1. Open the Material Editor. Select an unused material slot. Click **Standard** and pick **Multi/Sub-Object** from the Material/Map Browser. Click **Set Number** and set the number to 3.

2. For the first material, click the color swatch and change the color to a skin tone.

3. Copy this color to the color swatch for the third material. Change the color for the third material to a slightly darker or redder color, for the lips.

### Create Eye Material

The material for the eyes will take a bit more work as we need to create a special map to represent the eyeballs. You'll use a **Gradient Ramp** map to create a simple eye map from scratch.

1. Click the second material in the **Multi/Sub-Object** material.

2. For the Diffuse map, select the **Gradient Ramp** map.

3. Change the **Gradient Type** to **Radial**. Set up the gradient to include blue, black and white as shown in the picture.

The gradient works with small markers called *flags*. You can add a new flag by clicking on the gradient, or change a flag's color by double-clicking on it. The gradient ramp is created between adjacent color flags.

4. Click **Show Map in Viewport**.

The map doesn't show in viewports just yet because there are no mapping coordinates assigned to the eyes.

## Apply Mapping Coordinates

*Mapping coordinates* tell a map how to lie on the object. With a Gradient Ramp map, you have to tell the map how to align with the eyes. You do this with the **UVW Map** modifier.

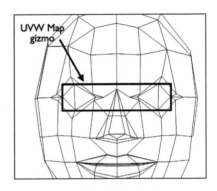

1. Select the polygons that make up the whites and pupils for each eye, four polygons in all. In the Front viewport, scale these polygons vertically a little bit to make the eyes bigger.

2. Without exiting the **Polygon** sub-object level, select the **MeshSmooth** modifier on the stack. Apply the **UVW Map** modifier at this level.

This will cause the **UVW Map** gizmo to fit itself to the eyes automatically.

3. Activate the Front viewport and click **View Align** on the command panel.

The **UVW Map** gizmo should now be positioned around the eyes, as shown in the picture. In addition, the eye map should now appear in shaded viewports.

☀ **TIP** ☀

*Try these values as a starting point for the Gradient Ramp values.*

*U Offset: 0*
*V Offset: 0.1*
*U Tile: 3*
*V Tile: 0.5*

4. Turn on **MeshSmooth** if it's not already on. Working with the smoothed model, adjust the **U** and **V Tiling** and **Offset** values for the **Gradient Ramp** map until the eyes are the correct size, and appear to look straight ahead in the Front viewport. You can also adjust the sizes of the black and blue areas of the gradient if necessary.

5. Save your work as **LPHead11.max**.

# CREATING THE HAIR

Low-poly hair can be created in a number of ways. This particular method uses a sphere, with extruded polygons representing tendrils or wisps of hair on the forehead.

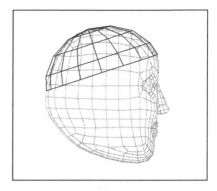

## Tutorial M27: CREATING THE HAIR

### Create the Hair Object

1. In the Top viewport, create a sphere about the size of the character's head. Set **Segments** to **16** and **Hemisphere** to **53**.

2. Move and rotate the sphere so it sits right on the character's head like a skull cap. Scale the sphere as necessary to make it closely fit the character's head.

3. Convert the sphere to an Editable Poly.

 4. Access the **Polygon** sub-object level.

5. Select all the polygons that make up the rounded portion of the sphere.

 6. Click the Bevel **Settings** button. Choose **Group** as the **Bevel Type**. Set **Height** to about **8** to make a helmet shape around the head, and click **OK** to exit the dialog.

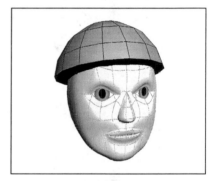

### Create Tendrils

1. Select three or four polygons on the flat part of the hemisphere near the character's face.

2. Use **Bevel** to extrude the polygons. Be sure to set the **Bevel Type** to **By Polygon** to cause the tendrils to separate as they extrude. Extrude twice so you have some polygons for bending the tendrils.

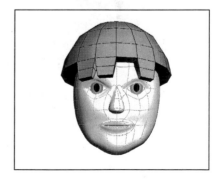

3. Use the **Vertex** or **Polygon** sub-object level to shape the wisps to look like clumps of hair brushed away from the face. You'll need to check your work in all viewports to ensure the wisps fall close to the head.

4. Select polygons on the flat part of the hemisphere around the sides and back of the head. Extrude these polygons to form the rest of the hair, using the **Group** method for the **Bevel Type** or **Extrusion Type**.

5. Shape the hair as you like. To check your work, apply the **MeshSmooth** modifier with **Iterations** set to 1 or **2**.

## Name Objects and Materials

1. Name the hair object **Hair**, and name the head object **Head**.

2. Apply an appropriate color or material to the hair.

3. In the Material Editor, select the head material. Click **Go to Parent** until you reach the root level of the material. Change the name of the material to **Head Material**.

4. If you applied a material to the hair, change the material name to **Hair Material**.

5. Save your work as **LPHead12.max**.

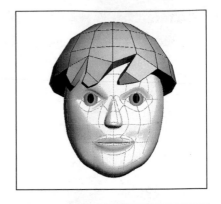

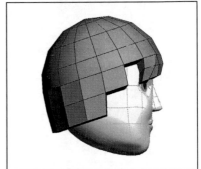

> ☼ **TIP** ☼
>
> *You can make the hair as long as you like by extruding a few more times.*

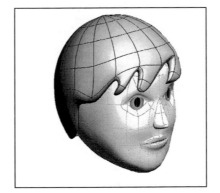

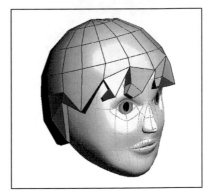

## MERGING

Now that you have a head and a body, you can merge the two. Merging will be a lot easier to deal with if we first name the objects appropriately.

## Tutorial M28: MERGING THE HEAD AND BODY

1. Load the latest **LPChar** file containing the character body.

2. Press **[M]** to open the Material Editor. Choose the body material, and name it **Body Material**.

3. Choose *File menu > Merge*, and choose the file **LPHead12.max**.

4. On the Merge dialog, select both the hair and head objects to merge them into the current file.

   The head and hair come into the current scene.

5. Position the head and hair on the body. Scale the head and hair if necessary.

6. If the fleshtone colors on the head and body don't match, adjust the materials in the Material Editor.

7. Turn on **MeshSmooth** to see how the materials look on the smoothed body.

8. Save your work as **LPCharFinal.max**.

## YOU MADE IT!

Congratulations! You have finished creating a low-poly character using both basic and advanced techniques in 3ds max. Feel free to learn more, experiment, and become a low-poly modeling expert.

# 2
# CHARACTER RIGGING

A *character rig* is a set of controls
that make the process of animation easier.

The primary element in a character rig is a bone structure that represents the skeleton for the character. When you animate the bones, the character mesh animates along with it.

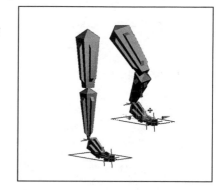

A rig can include helpers and shapes that help you control the bones. For example, you could set up control shapes that allow you to move the character's feet around easily and cause the knee to bend naturally.

You can also create custom parameters and set them up to affect different aspects of the rig. In this book, you'll create custom parameters to control the bending of the character's fingers, so you can make the character's hand form a fist just by changing a few values.

Ideally, a character rig should be set up in such a way that you can make the character perform all manner of actions with the controls alone. You should never have to animate any of the bones directly.

There are as many different kinds of character rigs as there are animators. In this book, you'll learn how to create a rig that uses a variety of controls. Along the way, you'll find out enough about rigging to create custom rigs for your own characters. You'll use the rig you create here to animate the character in the *Character Animation* chapter.

Part of the rigging process includes applying the Skin modifier to the mesh to associate the bones with it. You can apply the Skin modifier before setting up the character rig, or you can set up the character rig first. In this book, we'll set up the character rig before applying the Skin modifier in the *Skinning* chapter.

## TERMS AND CONCEPTS

Before we can talk about rigging, you'll need to understand a few concepts specific to the task.

### COORDINATE SYSTEMS

When you move, rotate, or scale an object, you use a set of XYZ axes that appear in viewports. The directions in which these axes point represent the current *reference coordinate system*, which is simply a method of referring to locations and directions in 3D space. These axes exist solely to make it easier for you to *transform* (move, rotate, scale) the objects in your scene.

### ☝ TIP ☝

The place where the X, Y and Z axes meet is referred to as the axes' origin point, or 0,0,0 point.

3ds max offers a number of coordinate systems that you can use at any time. Each one has a different way of determining which way the selected objects' axes will point.

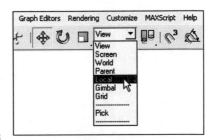

Changing the coordinate system doesn't change the objects in the scene in any way—it simply changes the axes that display when you select an object.

By default, the reference coordinate system is set to the *View* method. This method orients the XYZ axes depending on the active viewport. The X and Y axes are always perpendicular to the active viewport, except in Perspective or User viewports.

### ☝ TIP ☝

Each transform can have its own reference coordinate system. When you select a coordinate system, it is selected for the current transform only.

You can see the available coordinate systems on the Reference Coordinate System drop-down menu, which is located just to the right of the Select and Uniform Scale button on the Main Toolbar.

### LOCAL AXES

When you create an object, 3ds max assigns it a set of *local coordinates* or *local axes*. These axes rotate with the object.

 To see an object's local axes, rotate the object slightly, click Select and Move, and choose Local as the Reference Coordinate System. The directions of the local axes appear in viewports.

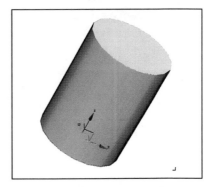

# LINKING

Linking creates a relationship between two objects, allowing you to control one object by moving or rotating the other.

In the illustration, box 2 is linked to box 1, and box 3 is linked to box 2.

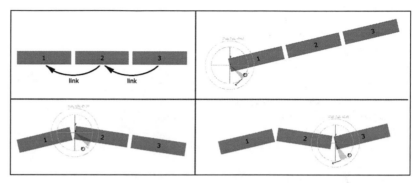

- **Rotate box 1:** All three boxes rotate.

- **Rotate box 2:** Boxes 2 and 3 rotate.

- **Rotate box 3:** Only box 3 rotates.

 Linking is a standard feature in 3ds max. You can link objects together using the Select and Link tool on the Main Toolbar.

Unlike attaching or grouping, linking allows the objects to move or rotate somewhat independently of one another.

One way to understand linking is to envision a stack of spools. If you glue the spools together end to end, you'll end up with a long, rigid stick. This approach can be likened to attaching or grouping the objects.

But if you loosely thread a piece of string through the spools instead, you'll end up with a flexible, whip-like object. Each spool can rotate independently of the others. This setup can be likened to the results of linking.

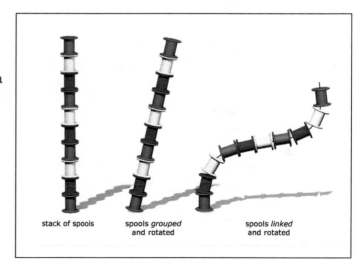

stack of spools    spools *grouped* and rotated    spools *linked* and rotated

The relationship between linked objects is called a *parent-child relationship*. You link the *child* to the *parent*. In the illustration at right, box 1 is a parent to box 2, while box 3 is a child of box 2.

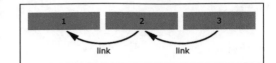

 To link objects with Select and Link, you drag from the child to the parent.

## BONES

A *bone* is a special type of object in 3ds max. When you create a series of bones, they're automatically linked together. In addition, you can automatically add animation controls to the chain as you create it. You'll use bones to form your character's skeleton, and provide the basis for the character rig.

 To access the bone creation tools, click the Systems button on the Create panel, and click Bones.

You will learn more about creating bones later in this chapter.

## CHAINS AND HIERARCHIES

A linear series of linked objects is called a *chain*.

You can also link two or more chains together to form a complex linked structure. Such a structure is called a *hierarchy*.

In every hierarchy, there is one object that is only a parent, and not a child to any other object. This object is called the *root* of the hierarchy. Every hierarchy has only one root.

There are two ways to create a chain or hierarchy in 3ds max:

 Create a series of ordinary objects such as primitives, and use Select and Link on the Main Toolbar to link them together.

 Create bones with Create panel > System > Bones.

---

## KINEMATICS

In the world of 3D animation, the term *kinematics* describes the movement of a linked structure. Depending on the type of kinematics you use, either the parent objects will control their children, or a child will control its parent.

With *forward kinematics*, when a parent in the chain moves or rotates, the children under it also move or rotate. This was the only method of kinematics available in the early days of computer animation, and it still has many uses. Forward kinematics is often referred to by its initials, *FK*.

With *inverse kinematics*, you can move a child object and have the parent objects rotate accordingly. For example, you could move a character's hand to cause the upper arm and lower arm to move and rotate appropriately. Inverse kinematics is usually called simply *IK*.

With IK, the root of the chain can rotate, but cannot move. In the scenario of the arm and hand, the upper arm is the root of the chain, so it rotates but doesn't move. By comparison, the lower arm can both move and rotate when the hand is moved.

IK is extremely useful for character animation. It takes a bit of work to set it up, but once it's in place, animation is easy and intuitive.

In this book, you'll learn how to use both FK and IK on a skeletal structure in 3ds max.

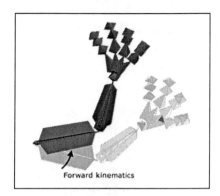

Forward kinematics

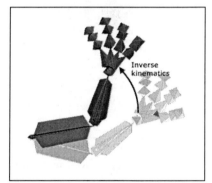

Inverse kinematics

## CHARACTER STRUCTURE

The diagram at right shows a humanoid skeleton made with five chains:

- Spine and head
- Two arms
- Two legs

In this book, you'll create five bone chains for your character, and link them together via custom control objects.

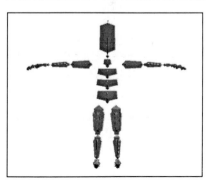

## BONE CREATION

To create bones, go to the Create panel and click the Systems button, which is all the way over at the right of the panel. Click Bones.

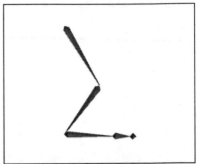

Click in any viewport, then move the cursor and click again. Continue to move the cursor and click to create more bones. When you've finished creating the chain, right-click to end bone creation.

As you create bones, they are linked in sequence. The first bone you create is the *root* (parent of all bones). The next is the child of the root, and so on down the line until you create the last child.

A number of options are available on the Create panel for bones. For example, you can automatically assign IK controls to the bones as you create them by checking Assign to Children on the IK Chain Assignment rollout before you create the bones. This option is useful if you're creating one chain to control a simple structure, but not necessarily useful for the complex hierarchy required for character animation.

In the exercises in this book, you won't assign IK controls automatically as you create bones. You'll learn more about IK chains later, when you create them manually for your bone structure.

After you create the bones, you can go to the Modify panel and change the Bone Parameters. These parameters change the width of the selected bone, and allow you to add fins. *Fins* are simply extrusions from the bone that help you visualize the bone's placement, and can help with the skinning process later on.

You can move the entire chain by moving the root bone. You can also move the chain by selecting all the bones and moving them all at once. Moving individual bones other than the root moves some of the bones, but not all of them.

By default, bones don't render in the scene. You can make them render by selecting all the bones, choosing *Edit menu > Object Properties*, and checking the Renderable checkbox on the Object Properties dialog.

In this exercise, you'll practice creating bones. The goal is to create a leg bone structure similar to one shown at right.

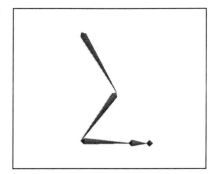

**Create One Leg**

To create bones, you will click once to start the leg structure, then click at each joint to set the bone. When you have finished, you will right-click to end the process.

1. Reset 3ds max by choosing *File menu > Reset.* Answer **Yes** when asked if you want to reset.

2. On the **Create** panel, click the **Systems** button.

3. Click **Bones**.

4. In the IK Chain Assignment rollout, make sure **Assign to Children** is unchecked.

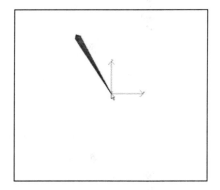

5. In the Left viewport, click near the top left of the viewport, then move the cursor down and slightly to the right, and click again.

   You have just created one bone.

6. Move the cursor down and to the left, and click again.

7. Move the cursor to the right to begin the foot bone, and click again.

8. Move the cursor further to the right to create the toe bone, and click again.

9. Right-click to end the bone creation process.

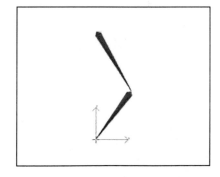

   The last click creates a small nub at the end of the toe. This small bone is necessary for character rigging.

   If you had difficulty creating the leg structure, delete the bones and try again. Keep practicing until you can easily create bone structures.

### Adjust the Bones

1. Use **Select and Move** to move different bones around. Note the following:

   - Moving the root moves the entire structure.

   - Moving a child causes its children to move with it, and causes its immediate parent to rotate.

   - The bones never change length, even when moved.

2. Select any bone and go to the **Modify** panel.

3. Adjust various parameters on the panel, and observe the results.

   Turning on any of the fin options creates extrusions from the sides of the bones. The fins can help you visualize the thickness of the mesh during the animation process.

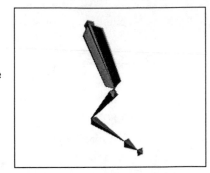

### Create a Hierarchy

You can make a hierarchy by creating a new chain of bones off an existing chain.

1. On the Create panel, click **Bones** again.

2. Click an existing bone, and start creating another chain.

   This will create a new chain off the first one, creating a hierarchy of two chains.

   You can save this scene if you like, but it is not necessary.

## BONE TOOLS

After you've created a bone structure, you might find you need to change the length of one or more of the bones. You can do this with Bone Tools.

Choose *Character menu > Bone Tools*. The Bone Tools dialog appears.

There are many things you can do with bones on this dialog. For now, we'll focus on changing the length of a bone.

On the Bone Tools dialog, click Bone Edit Mode. Select a bone in the middle of the chain, and use Select and Move to move it around.

As you move the bone, it becomes longer or shorter, and its parent changes length accordingly. Compare this with moving the bone when Bone Edit Mode is turned off, which rotates the bone but does not change its length.

When Bone Edit Mode is on, the root bone behaves a little differently from the others. It becomes longer or shorter but doesn't affect its parent, since it doesn't have one.

The last child object, the nub at the end of the chain, doesn't change in length as you move it. It does, however, affect the length of its parent bone.

On the Bone Tools dialog, you can also create or adjust fins for several bones at once on the Fin Adjustment Tools rollout.

## Practice H: EDITING BONES WITH BONE TOOLS

For this practice, you can use the bones you created earlier, or create a new chain.

1. Choose *Character menu > Bone Tools.*

2. On the Bone Tools dialog, turn on **Bone Edit Mode**.

3. Practice changing the lengths of bones to understand how this tool works.

4. Turn off **Bone Edit Mode**.

5. Expand the Fin Adjustment Tools rollout.

6. Select several bones. Change the fin options and observe the result.

   Be sure to turn on **Side Fins**, **Front Fin**, or **Back Fin** to make the fins appear.

7. In the Bone Objects group, change the **Width** and **Height** parameters. Observe the result.

   The **Width** and **Height** parameters change the bone's dimensions without changing its length.

8. Change the **Taper** parameter and observe the result.

   The **Taper** parameter affects the degree to which the bone narrows from the parent end to the child end.

   You can save this scene if you like, but it is not necessary.

## WHERE DO YOU PUT THE BONES?

In the next tutorial, you will begin to create the bones for the character. Ideally, you should place each set of bones right at the center of the corresponding part of the model. For example, the bones for the right leg should run down the center of the character's right leg and foot. The bones for the spine should be placed at the center of the character's torso.

After you create bones, you can adjust them and move them around if necessary. This takes a little time, but it's well worth it in the end. Well-placed bones make it easy to apply the Skin modifier and animate the character, while badly-placed bones turn the animation process into a nightmare. If you try to fix the bones after applying Skin, you'll make a mess of your character mesh.

> ### ☀ TIP ☀
> *Professional riggers always complete the rig before applying the Skin modifier to the character mesh.*

## Tutorial R1: CREATING THE LEG BONES

In this exercise, you'll create a bone structure for your character. If you haven't done so already, create a folder on your hard disk named *Rigs* to hold your character rig files.

The rigging exercises shown here create a rig for the *Skater_Char.max* character from the *Characters* folder on the CD. If you like, you can use the character you created earlier in this book, or another character from the CD. If this is your first time creating a character rig, I strongly recommend that you use a simple humanoid character, and not an alien, monster or animal. Later, after you've gone through the process once, you can apply what you've learned to a more complicated character.

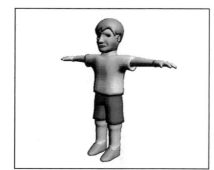

At any point during this exercise, you can load the rigging file from the CD to see how it's done. For example, if the exercise tells you to save the file **CharRig12.max**, you can load this file from the CD as an example.

### Prepare the Character for Rigging

1. Load the the character you created earlier in this book, or load the file *Characters/Skater_Char.Max* from the CD.

    *Important:* If you're using your own model, make sure the character is facing the Front viewport, and rotate it if necessary. Otherwise, some of the steps in this tutorial might not work as expected.

2. If any parts of the character have a **MeshSmooth** modifier applied to them, remove the modifier. To do this, select the object, go to the **Modify** panel, highlight **MeshSmooth** on the stack, and click **Remove modifier from the stack**.

    The character might look a little strange without **MeshSmooth**, but it will be much easier for you to rig the character this way. You can apply **MeshSmooth** again later, after the rig is done.

3. Select all parts of the character.

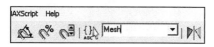

4. Create a Named Selection Set called **Mesh**. To do this, enter **Mesh** in the **Named Selection Set** area on the Main Toolbar.

    The term *mesh* is another name for a model. In a 3D scene, the named selection set **Mesh** will distinguish the model from other objects in the scene, such as bones and rig controls.

When you perform the rigging tasks, your job will be much easier if the character is aligned with the construction grid.

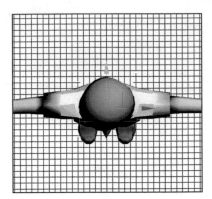

5. In the Front viewport, press the **[G]** key to display the construction grid, if it is not already displayed. Move the character so it is standing on the construction grid.

6. In the Top viewport, turn on the grid if necessary, and move the character in any viewport so it is centered on the Y axis.

   If you prefer to work with the grid turned off, you can turn it off with the **[G]** key after you've finished aligning the character with the construction plane.

   It will be easier to set up the rig if you make the character see-through, and freeze it.

7. Press **[Alt-X]** on the keyboard to make the character see-through.

8. Right-click in any viewport to access the Quad menu, and choose *Freeze Selection*.

9. If you like, change the display for each viewport to a shaded view. To do this, right-click the viewport label and choose *Smooth+Highlights* from the pop-up menu.

**Create the First Leg Structure**

1. In the Left viewport, zoom in on the character's legs.

2. Choose **Create panel > Systems > Bones**.

3. In the IK Chain Assignment rollout, make sure **Assign to Children** is unchecked.

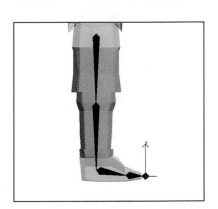

4. Starting near the character's hip, create a bone structure for the leg with thigh, calf, foot, and toe. The click for the end of the toe should be right at the tip of the character's foot. Right-click to end bone creation.

   Don't be concerned if your leg bones aren't exactly right for your character's legs, or if they don't match the picture exactly.

### Adjust Bone Lengths

Look at the leg bones only in the Left viewport for now. If the leg bones match the character's leg when viewed in the Left viewport, and if the nub sticks out past the end of the foot, you can skip this set of steps.

1. Choose *Character menu > Bone Tools*.

2. In the Bone Tools dialog, click **Bone Edit Mode**.

3. In the Left viewport, adjust the lengths and positions of the leg bones until they fit inside the character's leg.

4. Move the toe nub so it begins at the tip of the character's foot.

5. Turn off **Bone Edit Mode**.

### Move the Leg Bones

Now that the bones match the character in the Left viewport, you can work on matching them in the Front viewport.

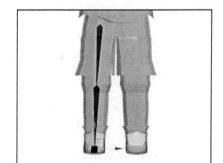

1. In the Front viewport, move the root bone (thigh bone) so the top of it sits at the center of the character's right hip. Don't look at the rest of the bones—work with just the top of the thigh for now. Zoom into the viewport if necessary to get the placement just right.

2. Move the calf bone so the knee joint matches the character's right knee.

3. If this makes the thigh bone so short that it doesn't reach the knee area, choose *Character menu > Bone Tools* and turn on **Bone Edit Mode**, then move the calf bone downward to make the thigh bone longer. Turn off **Bone Edit Mode** when you're done. You can leave the Bone Tools dialog open while you continue, as long as **Bone Edit Mode** is turned off while you're moving the bones into place.

4. In the Left viewport, select the foot bone.

5. In the Front viewport, move the foot bone until the calf bone goes down the center of the character's right calf.

6. If this makes the calf bone too short, use **Bone Edit Mode** to move the foot bone into the character's foot, which will lengthen the calf.

7. Check the placement of the bones in all viewports, and make any necessary adjustments.

Study the relationship between the bones and the character carefully in both the Front and Left viewports. Make sure the bones run down the center of the leg and foot before continuing.

## Name the Leg Bones

Naming objects and bones properly is a very important part of character rigging. If you don't name your bones, your scene will become confusing to you later on.

For some reason, no one likes to take the time to name the objects in their scene. This step will take less than two minutes, but will save you a lot of time and frustration later on.

1. Name the bones as follows, starting from the root:

   - **BoneThighR**
   - **BoneCalfR**
   - **BoneFootR**
   - **BoneToeR**
   - **BoneToeNubR**

2. Save the scene in your *Rigs* folder with the filename **CharRig01.max**.

## Create Fins

Fins are extrusions from bones. During the animation process, you'll probably have the character mesh hidden, and you'll only be able to see the bones. In this case, fins can be very handy for helping you visualize the character's dimensions.

The goal in creating fins is to increase the width of the bone until the fins fill up about ¾ of the character mesh at that point. Adjusting fins is not an exact science; it's far more important to center the bones on the mesh than is to make the fins a particular size.

1. Select all the bones except the toe nub.

2. If the Bone Tools dialog isn't already open, choose *Character menu > Bone Tools*.

3. Check the **Side Fins**, **Front Fin** and **Back Fin** options.

   This creates fins with the default size of 5.

4. Select the thigh bone only.

☙ **TIP** ☙

*The **R** at the end of each bone name stands for "right". You should always name the bones for the character's side of the body, not the side that you see in the Front viewport. This ensures that you'll always know which side of the body each part refers to regardless of the camera angle, or how much the character turns during the animation.*

☙ **TIP** ☙

*There are as many different naming conventions as there are animators. In this book, we put the object type first, then the body part, then the side of the body. Some animators prefer to use all lowercase letters except for the right/left designation, for example bonethighR. Some prefer to put the right/left designation first and put the body part in capital letters, as in rTHIGHbone.*

*In your own work, it doesn't matter what convention you use as long as you're consistent. Using the same naming convention for multiple characters makes it easier to keep track of what you're doing, and also makes it easy to transfer animation from one character to another.*

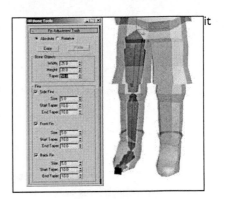

5. In the Bone Objects group on the Bone Tools dialog, change the parameters to the following:

**Width**    **25**
**Height**    **30**
**Taper**    **50**

The bone should fill out approximately ¾ of the character mesh at each part, so these fins will be sufficient for the character's thigh.

6. Select each bone except the toe nub, and for each one, adjust the **Width**, **Height** and **Taper** values so each bone fills about ¾ of the mesh around it.

7. Save the scene in your *Rigs* folder with the filename **CharRig02.max**.

You can quickly save the file with this name by choosing *File Menu > Save As* and clicking **[+]** on the dialog.

## Mirror the Leg Bones

Now that you have one leg set up correctly, you can mirror the leg bones to the other side of the character's body.

1. In the Front viewport, select all the leg bones.

2. On the Main Toolbar, click **Mirror Selected Objects**. You can also choose *Tools menu > Mirror*.

3. In the Mirror dialog, choose **X** as the **Mirror Axis**.

4. For **Clone Selection**, choose **Copy**, and click **OK** to close the dialog.

5. If necessary, move the mirrored bones until they are centered on the character's left leg.

*Note:* If you created your character with the **Symmetry** modifier, the left leg bones should fit perfectly inside the character's left leg with no further adjustments. If your character is asymmetrical, you might have to adjust the left leg bones to fit the character's leg.

6. Change the names of the left leg bones to **BoneThighL**, **BoneCalfL**, **BoneFootL**, **BoneToeL**, and **BoneToeNubL**.

7. Save your scene as **CharRig03.max**.

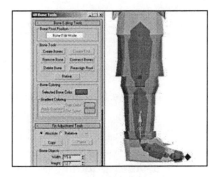

### ☙ TIP ☙

*You can make the foot bone fill the center of the foot by turning on Bone Edit Mode and moving the foot bone upward a little, as shown in the image above. This will also move the pivot point between the calf and foot closer to the ankle, which will make your animation more accurate.*

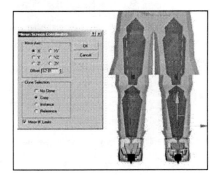

### ☙ TIP ☙

*By setting the fins and bone dimensions before mirroring the bones, you saved yourself the trouble of having to set these parameters again for the left leg bones.*

## Tutorial R2: Creating the Spine Bones

The bones for the spine will go right up into the neck and head.

### Create the Bones

1. Load the file *CharRig03.max* you created earlier, or load this file from the CD.

   Next, you will create the spine bones. The logical thing would be to create them up the center of the character's back, but this can cause a problem. When you click near the base of the spine, the new bones will try to attach themselves to the thigh bones. We want the spine to remain separate, and then we'll rig it to the legs later.

   To do this, you'll create the bones just behind the character's back, away from the existing bones. Later, you'll move the spine bones into place.

2. Go to **Create panel > Systems > Bones**.

3. In the Left viewport, create bones up the character's back. Start behind the hips and work upward, creating four bones for the back, one for the neck, and one for the head. Right-click to create the nub and end bone creation.

   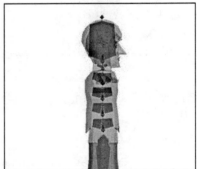

4. In the Left and Front viewports, move the bone at the base of the spine to the center of the character's hips.

### Finish the Bones

1. Choose *Character menu > Bone Tools*. For each spine bone, adjust fins to make each bone fill about ¾ of the character mesh. Close the Bone Tools dialog when you have finished.

   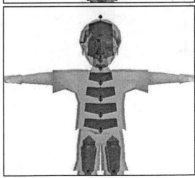

2. Name the spine bones as follows, starting from the lowest spine bone:

   - **BoneSpine01**
   - **BoneSpine02**
   - **BoneSpine03**
   - **BoneSpine04**
   - **BoneNeck**
   - **BoneHead**
   - **BoneHeadnub**

3. Save the scene as **CharRig04.max**.

# Tutorial R3: Creating Arm and Hand Bones

The arm bones require several parts: a clavicle, the arm bones, and several bones for the fingers.

A *clavicle* is a bone in your shoulder that controls the shoulder's rotation. You will use it to animate the shoulders when the character's arm moves up or down a great deal. This bone might seem unimportant, but leaving it out will cause the resulting animation to appear stiff and unnatural around the shoulders.

### Create the Arm Bones

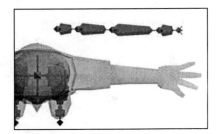

1. Continue with the scene you just used, or load the file *CharRig04.max* from the *Rigs* folder on the CD.

2. Go to **Create panel > Systems**, and click **Bones**.

3. Turn on **Side Fins**, **Front Fin**, and **Back Fin**.

   Turning on these options before creating the bones will cause the bones to be created with fins automatically.

4. In the Top viewport, create five bones and a nub. Start at the neck area and create a clavicle, then create an upper arm bone, a lower arm bone, and a palm bone. Right-click to end bone creation and create a nub at the end of the chain.

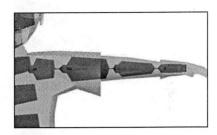

5. In the Top and Front viewports, move the upper arm bone to move the entire arm structure to sit inside the character's arm.

6. Choose *Character menu > Bone Tools*. Use Bone Tools to adjust the lengths of the bones, and adjust the fin sizes as necessary. Check your work in the Front and Left viewports. Be sure to turn off **Bone Edit Mode** when you have finished.

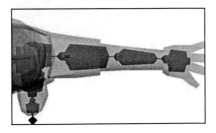

   The nub allowed you to create a palm bone and easily adjust its length by moving the nub. But you won't need it for the rig, and it will only get in the way, so you can delete it.

7. Delete the nub at the end of the chain.

8. Name the bones as follows:

- **BoneClavicleL**
- **BoneUpperArmL**
- **BoneLowerArmL**
- **BonePalmL**

☙ **TIP** ☙

*If you make the lower arm bone bend slightly in the appropriate direction, it will be easier to set up the arm rig later on.*

## Create the Finger Bones

Next you will create finger bones and link them to the palm bone.

1. In the Top viewport, zoom in on the left hand.

2. Go to **Create panel > Systems**, and click **Bones**. Turn off the fin options for all the bones.

3. In the Top viewport, create the bones for the pinky. Move the cursor to the base of the pinky finger, then click to set the first bone. Click twice more to create the bones along the finger, then right-click to end bone creation and create the finger nub.

   Take care not to link the pinky to the palm bone as you create the new bone structure. If you do so, the bone will begin at the center of the hand. If this happens, undo bone creation and try again.

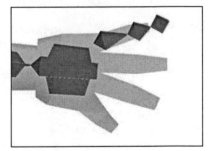

4. Create similar chains for the middle finger and index finger.

   As you create the bones, if they try to connect to the palm upon creation, try creating the bone structure away from the hand and moving it into place afterward by moving the base finger bone.

5. Create the bone structure for the thumb.

   Note that the base thumb bone begins halfway down the hand. If you look at your own thumb bone, you will see that its rotation actually begins close to the wrist. Placing the bone in this way will make it possible to animate the thumb more realistically.

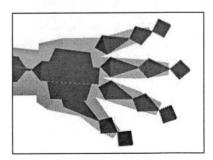

6. If necessary, move the bones in the Front viewport so they sit inside the character's hand.

If you look at the finger bones in the Front viewport, you will see that they go straight ahead while the character's fingers bend. You will make the finger bones bend to match the character's fingers when you set up the finger controls later on.

7. Name the finger bones as shown in the illustration below.

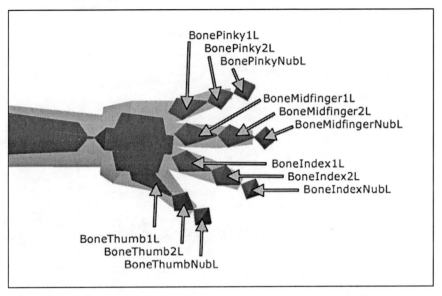

This might seem like a lot of bones to name. But it will only take five to ten minutes to name them, and the names will help you a great deal when you set up the rig for the fingers.

8. Link each of the finger base bones (the bones with the suffix **1L**) to the palm bone.

9. Save the scene as **CharRig05.max**.

## Mirror the Arm

Strictly speaking, this procedure is optional. Later, you will rig one arm and mirror the entire rig, bones and all, to the other side.

However, it can be very satisfying to see the entire bone structure in place. This procedure takes just a few minutes, and it will enable you to see the entire bone structure and its relationship to the mesh. It will also give you practice in renaming objects.

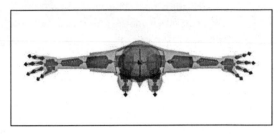

1. Select all parts of the arm and hand, including the clavicle and fingers.

2. Change the **Reference Coordinate System** to **World**.

3. In the Main Toolbar, set the transform coordinate center to **Use Transform Coordinate Center**.

4. Use **Mirror Selected Objects** to mirror and copy the arm to the other side of the body, using **X** as the **Mirror Axis**.

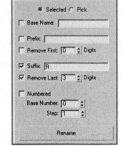

   If you aligned the character with the construction grid earlier, the mirrored arm should be nearly in the right place. Move it if necessary.

5. Check the alignment of the finger bones in the Top viewport. If the character is not perfectly symmetrical, you might have to adjust the arm or finger bones to make them fit properly.

6. Change the names of the right hand bones to the same as those for the left, but with an **R** on the end instead of an **L**.

   To quickly rename all the objects, press **[H]** on the keyboard to display a list of the objects in the scene, and type ***L01** in the entry area at the top of the Select Objects dialog to display all the newly copied bones. Click **Select** to select them. Then choose *Tools menu > Rename Objects*. On the Rename Object dialog, choose **Selected**. Turn on **Suffix** and **Remove Last**, and turn off all other options. Enter **R** for **Suffix**, and set the **Remove Last** number to **3**. Click **Rename** once, and close the dialog. The bones will be renamed with the letter **R** instead of **L01**.

   If you want to see how the structure is linked, press the **[H]** key to open the Select Objects dialog, and check **Display Subtree** at the bottom of the dialog. Child bones are displayed as indented below their parent objects.

7. Select all the bones, and create a named selection set called **Bones**.

8. Save the scene as **CharRig06.max**.

   The bone structure is complete. Now you can get on to the task of setting up controls for the rig.

# IK CHAINS

An *IK chain* is a control object that allows you to manipulate bones with the IK method.

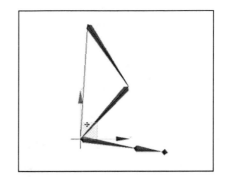

Recall that inverse kinematics (IK) allows you to control an entire chain by moving a child in the chain. For example, you'll be able to control the thigh and calf by moving one IK chain at the heel.

The IK chain is created as an object called IK Chain01 that appears as a set of crosshairs and a line connecting the starting and ending bones. You can select an IK chain like any other object, but it doesn't render.

An IK chain has special properties. When you select an IK chain, the crosshairs are the part that's really selected. The line that appears between the starting and ending bones is just a display, so you can see where the chain starts and ends.

The IK chain isn't "linked" to the bones in the usual sense of linking, nor are the bones linked to the IK chain. The movement of the bones, however, depends on the animation of the IK chain.

You can create an IK chain by selecting the first bone you want to use in the chain, choosing *Animation menu > IK Solvers > HI Solver*, then clicking the last bone for the chain.

 An IK chain is different from any other object in 3ds max. It's not like a box or a sphere, or even like bones. If you select an IK chain and go to the Modify panel, there's nothing there to modify. All the controls for an IK chain are on the Motion panel.

## Practice J: CREATING AN IK CHAIN

1. Reset 3ds max.

2. Create a quick set of leg bones to use for practice.

3. Select the root of the chain, which is the thigh bone in this case.

4. Choose *Animation menu > IK Solver > HI Solver*, then click the foot bone.

   Just before you click, a dotted line appears from the thigh to the foot. After a moment, the IK chain is created. You can see it as a line extending from the top of the thigh to the heel, and a set of crosshairs at the heel.

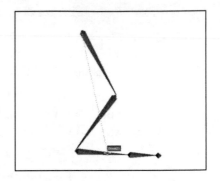

 5. Use **Select and Move** to move the crosshairs. The foot moves with the crosshairs, and the knee bends to accommodate the motion.

6. Turn on **Auto Key**, and set keys for the crosshairs on different frames.

   Fun, isn't it? You could probably spend all day playing with this one leg. But there are more adventures in store, so let's move along.

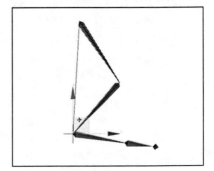

7. Save your work as **Practice_IkChain01.max**.

   Now that you have an idea of how an IK chain works, let's go over a few of the concepts that go with it.

## IK SOLVERS

When you moved the IK chain's crosshairs around, it actually moved the foot first, then calculated how the thigh and calf should rotate to accommodate the movement. It had to decide whether to bend the knee forward, backward or sideways, and it had to figure out by how much to bend the knee to make the foot go where you placed it.

In other words, the IK chain had to "solve" the problem of how the knee should bend. These calculations are figured out by an *IK solver*. The result is called an *IK solution*.

The IK chain's crosshairs represent a *goal* for the IK solution. When you move the goal, the chain of bones come up with a solution so the end of the last bone in the IK chain can meet the goal.

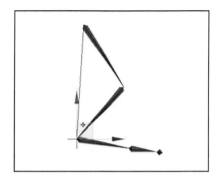

## THE HI SOLVER

Recall that you set up the IK chain by choosing *Animation menu > IK Solver > HI Solver*. An IK solver is a general name for the different types of IK chains you can set up and use.

The HI solver (history-independent solver) is the type of IK solver you'll use in this book. You can find a detailed explanation of its history and usage in the 3ds max documentation, accessible from the *Help* menu. Here, I will simply state that it's the most versatile and useful one for character animation.

Part of the IK solution involves figuring out which way the bend will point. If you create the bones in a "bent" state, the HI solver will consider that the default bending direction. However, you can make the bend point in a different direction by changing the IK solver's *swivel angle*. To change the swivel angle, select the IK chain and go to the Motion panel. The Swivel Angle parameter is on the IK Solver Properties rollout.

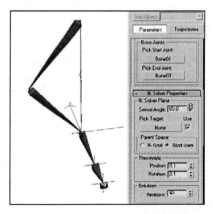

To gain better control over a chain of bones, you can create more than one HI solver on a chain of bones. Multiple HI solvers on a single chain are necessary for most character rigs.

Here, you'll practice creating multiple IK chains on the same bone chain.

**Create a Toe IK Chain**

1. Load the file **Practice_IkChain01.max** that you created earlier, if it's not still on your screen. You can also load this file from the *Practice* folder on the CD.

2. In the Left viewport, zoom in on the leg structure so you can easily see all the bones.

3. Select the foot bone.

4. Choose *Animation menu* > *IK Solvers* > *HI Solver*, and click the nub at the end of the toe.

Now there are two IK chains on the leg.

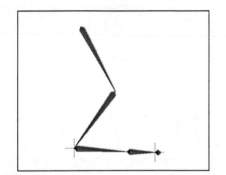

**Move the IK Chains**

1. Use **Select and Move** to select the IK chain at the heel, and move it around.

The toe stays put while the heel moves. It's okay if the toe bends in the wrong direction—we're just practicing right now.

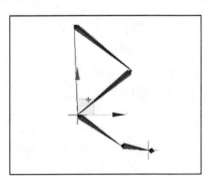

2. Undo the movement of the heel that you just made.

3. Select the IK chain at the toe, and move it around. The toe moves all by itself.

4. Undo the movement of the toe that you just made.

**Make the Entire Foot Move at Once**

The way the IK chains are set up now, you'd have to select both IK chains to make the entire foot move at once. However, you can simplify things by linking one IK chain to another, so you only have to move one chain to move the entire foot.

1. Select the heel IK chain.

2. On the Main Toolbar, click **Select and Link**. Click and drag from the heel IK chain to the toe IK chain.

The heel IK chain is now linked to the toe IK chain.

---

3. Select and move the toe IK chain.

   Now the entire foot moves when you move the toe.

4. Undo any movements you just made.

5. Select and move the heel IK chain.

   The heel still moves independently of the toe.

   This is a better rig, but it still has a problem. Every time you move the heel, the toe bends or flexes. Animators call this type of bend a *foot roll*, since it's the type of "rolling" action a back foot makes just before coming off the ground to take a step. Foot roll is necessary when you're animating a walk or a run, but only when the foot is about to come off the ground. The foot usually doesn't make this motion when it is in the air.

   You can still get some animation out of a rig like the one you've just created, but it would make things unnecessarily difficult for you. Every time you want to raise the heel but not roll the foot, you'd have to be very careful to always keep the heel far enough away from the toe to prevent a mid-air foot roll.

   Fortunately, there is a solution. You can prevent unwanted foot roll by adding yet another IK chain.

6. Undo any movements you've made before continuing.

**Control the Foot Roll**

1. Select the toe IK chain, and delete it.

2. Select the foot bone. Choose *Animation menu > IK Solvers > HI Solver*, and click the toe bone (not the nub, but the toe itself).

   You might wonder why you're making an IK chain that simply goes from one bone to the next. The answer is, because it makes it easier to control each part of the foot. Let's make another one.

3. Select the toe bone. Choose *Animation menu > IK Solvers > HI Solver*, and click the toe nub bone.

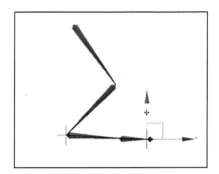

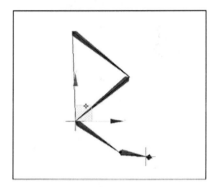

If you try moving any of these IK chains, the foot motion won't be very good. You'll need to link them together before you can get any decent results.

For the purposes of explanation, we'll call the IK chains the heel, middle and toe IK chains, in that order.

4. Use **Select and Link** to link the heel IK chain to the middle IK chain.

5. Link the middle IK chain to the toe IK chain.

6. Select and move the toe IK chain. The entire foot moves.

7. Select the middle IK chain, and rotate it. The heel comes up off the ground, and the foot rolls only exactly as much as you want it to.

   This is an added bonus of linking IK chains together—you can rotate the child IK chain by rotating the parent.

## Adjust the Swivel Angle

Every HI solver has its own **Swivel Angle** parameter. Here, you will locate the parameter and play with it to see how it works. You will need to understand this parameter to set up your character rig.

1. Select the IK chain at the heel.

2. Go to the **Motion** panel.

3. On the IK Solver Properties rollout, locate the **Swivel Angle** parameter. Change the **Swivel Angle** to change the direction in which the knee points.

4. Select other IK chains in the scene, and adjust their **Swivel Angle** parameters to see what happens.

5. Save your work as **Practice_IkChain02.max**.

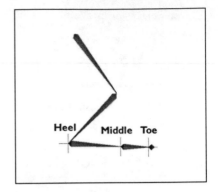

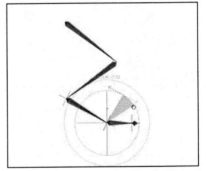

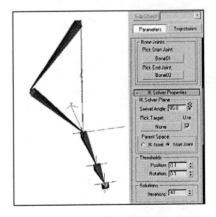

## Tutorial R4: Creating IK Chains for the Legs

Now you're ready to create the IK chains for your character rig. You'll use the same setup you created in the previous practice exercise.

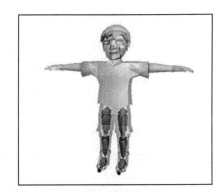

### Load and Hide the Character Mesh

1. Load the file *CharRig06.max* that you created earlier, or load it from the *Rigs* folder on the CD.

   You won't need the mesh for this part of the rigging process, so you can hide it. First you'll have to unfreeze it.

2. Right-click any viewport to display the Quad menu, and choose *Unfreeze All*.

3. Use the *Named Selection Sets* dropdown menu to choose the *Mesh* set.

4. Right-click any viewport, and choose *Hide Selection* from the Quad menu.

5. Select and hide all the bones for the upper body, leaving just the legs and feet.

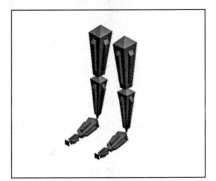

### Create the IK Chains

1. If your lower right viewport displays a Perspective view, change it to a User view. You can do this quickly by activating the Perspective view and clicking the **[U]** key on the keyboard.

2. In the User viewport, use **Arc Rotate** to adjust the viewport to an angle where you can clearly see and select all the bones in the both legs. Zoom into the viewport if necessary.

3. Select the right calf. In the Left viewport, rotate the calf so it bends backward, like a normal human knee.

   This bend will help the IK chain figure out which way the knee should bend. If you leave the bones straight when you create the IK chain, the knee might bend in any direction.

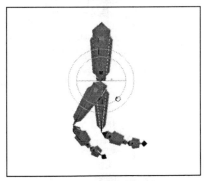

4. Select the right thigh bone. Choose *Animation menu > IK Solvers > HI Solver* and click the right foot bone.

5. Use the new IK chain to move the leg back into its original position. You can use the Left viewport to help you match the left leg's position to the right leg.

6. Create an IK chain from the right foot to the toe, and from the toe to the nub.

7. Rotate the left calf to bend the knee, and do the same steps for the left leg to create three IK chains for that leg.

## Name the IK Chains

IK chains can be named like any other object. Simply select the IK chain by clicking the crosshairs, then change the name on the **Modify** panel.

1. Go to the **Modify** panel.

2. Select and rename each IK chain to the names shown in the diagram at right.

The middle IK chain is named IKBallL or IKBallR for the ball of the foot, which is the name for the pad just below the toes.

## Link the Chains Together

1. In the User viewport, zoom in on the feet.

2. For each foot, use **Select and Link** to link the heel IK chain to the ball IK chain, and the ball IK chain to the toe IK chain. More specifically, link the IK chains together as follows:

   - Link **IKHeelR** to **IKBallR**

   - Link **IKBallR** to **IKToeR**

   - Link **IKHeelL** to **IKBallL**

   - Link **IKBallL** to **IKToeL**

3. To check your linkages, click Select Objects, then press the [H] key to display the Select Objects dialog. Check the **Display Subtree** checkbox at the bottom of the dialog. The linkages will display with child objects indented beneath their parents.

4. If the linkages don't match the dialog shown at right, select all the IK chains, click **Unlink Selection** on the Main Toolbar to remove the linkages, and link them together again.

5. Save the scene as **CharRig07.max**.

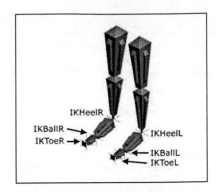

> ☙ **TIP** ☙
>
> *Naming IK chains is just as important as naming bones.*

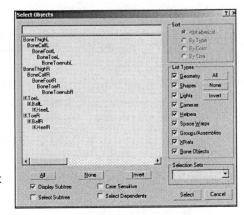

> ☙ **TIP** ☙
>
> *You might wonder why we didn't add the IK chains to just one leg and mirror the entire setup to the other side. This wouldn't work because IK chains don't always copy or mirror reliably. There's no problem with mirroring bones alone, but if you mirror and copy a bone structure with IK chains on it, the copied structure might not animate as expected.*

## CUSTOMIZATION TOOLS

When you start animating a character, the situation can quickly become unwieldy. To illustrate this concept, let's consider the character's legs.

To lift the foot and bend the leg, you can move the IK chain at the heel. That's easy, so there's no big problem there.

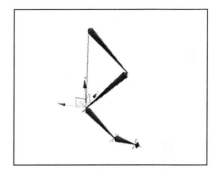

But suppose you want to animate the character to stand on tip-toe. You would have to rotate the foot and toe IK chains individually. Then, if you wanted to swivel the knee outward, you would have to animate the IK chain's swivel angle.

Imagine having to select each of these controls and animate them separately. Now imagine doing this for a long animation. You would quickly become frustrated. And that's just the legs! The situation would be compounded as you animated the spine, head, arms, and fingers.

This is where customization tools come in. *Custom attributes* and *parameter wiring* are two important customization tools that professional riggers use all the time. In this book, you will learn to use them for your character rig.

### CUSTOM ATTRIBUTES

A *custom attribute* is a parameter you can add to any object in the scene. Custom attributes don't do anything on their own, but you can make them control other parameters. Custom attributes are very handy for controlling different parts of a character rig.

To add a custom attribute to an object, select the object and choose *Animation menu > Add Custom Attribute*. The Add Parameter dialog appears. Here you set the parameter type, name and range.

 When you add a custom attribute to an object, it appears on the Modify panel along with all the object's usual parameters. Then you can connect the custom attribute to another value used in the character rig.

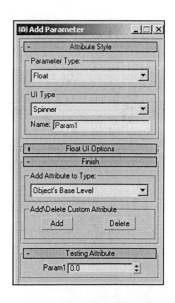

## PARAMETER WIRING

*Parameter wiring* connects, or wires, one value in the scene to another.

For example, you could wire a custom attribute to the rotation of an object in the scene, such as an IK chain. When you change the custom parameter, it will rotate the IK chain. This saves you from having to rotate the IK chain manually.

Parameter wiring is very handy for character rigging. In this book, you will use parameter wiring extensively to rig the character.

Parameter wiring is accomplished with the Parameter Wiring dialog. You can open this dialog several ways:

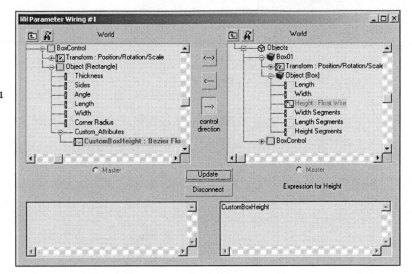

- Choose *Animation menu > Wire Parameters > Parameter Wire Dialog*.

- Choose *Animation menu > Wire Parameters > Wire Parameters,* and click the objects and parameters you want to wire.

- Right-click a selected object and choose *Wire Parameters* from the Quad menu, and click the objects and parameters you want to wire.

The use of the custom attributes with parameter wiring is illustrated in the next practice exercise.

In this practice exercise, you'll create a custom attribute for a box, and wire it to the box's height. Then you will change the box's height using the custom attribute.

### Create a Box

1. Reset 3ds max.

2. In the Top or Perspective viewport, create a box with a **Length**, **Width** and **Height** of 40 units.

3. On the **Create** panel, click **Shapes**, then click **Rectangle**.

4. In the Top viewport, create a small rectangle, and place it next to the box. Name the rectangle **BoxControl**.

### Add a Custom Attribute

1. Select **BoxControl**.

2. Go to the **Modify** panel.

3. Choose *Animation menu > Add Custom Attribute*.

   The Add Parameter dialog appears.

   Under the Parameter Type dropdown menu are several options. The default type is **Float**. This simply means a number that can have decimal places. We want the custom attribute to be set as this type of number, so leave the Parameter Type set to **Float**.

4. Change the **Name** to **CustomBoxHeight**.

5. Expand the Float UI Options rollout, and set the **Range** to go from **0** to **500**.

6. In the Finish rollout, click **Add**.

   On the **Modify** panel, you can see the new parameter **CustomBoxHeight** in the new Custom Attributes rollout.

7. Close the Add Parameter dialog by clicking the **[X]** at its upper right corner.

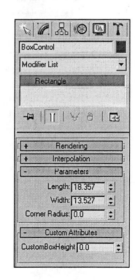

## Wire the Custom Attribute

If you change the **CustomBoxHeight** value on the **Modify** panel, nothing happens. That's because the value hasn't been wired to anything yet.

1. Choose *Animation menu > Wire Parameters > Parameter Wire Dialog* to open the Parameter Wiring dialog.

   On each side of the dialog are listings of different aspects of the scene. You can expand the listings by clicking the **[+]** to the left of each type of scene element. Here, we are interested in the listings under **Objects**.

2. On the left side of the dialog, expand the listing for **Objects** if it isn't already expanded.

3. Continue to expand the listings as follows: **BoxControl > Object (Rectangle) > Custom Attributes**.

   Expanding the **Custom Attributes** listing shows all the object's custom attributes. In this case, there is only one custom attribute, **CustomBoxHeight**.

4. Highlight the **CustomBoxHeight** listing.

5. On the right side of the dialog, expand the listing for **Objects > Box01 > Object (Box)**, and highlight the **Height** listing.

   Now that the parameters are highlighted, you need to tell the dialog the direction of the wiring. In this case, you want the parameter on the left (the custom attribute) to control the parameter on the right (the box's height).

6. Click the right arrow button at the center of the dialog.

   This says that you want the wiring to go from left to right.

7. Click **Connect**.

   Now the parameters are wired. Don't be concerned when the box becomes completely flat. The custom attribute is currently set to 0, so the box becoming flat means the wiring is working.

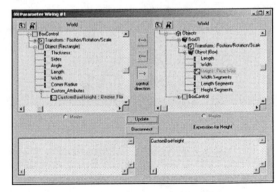

### Test the Wiring

When you connected the two parameters, the box went completely flat. This is because the custom attribute is set to 0, so the box's height went to 0 as well.

1. Close the Parameter Wiring dialog.

2. Select **BoxControl**, the rectangle.

3. On the **Modify** panel, increase the **CustomBoxHeight** value.

   If the box's height increases as you increase the **CustomBoxHeight** value, the wiring is working properly.

4. Save the scene as **Practice_CA01.max**.

   The **CA** stands for **C**ustom **A**ttribute.

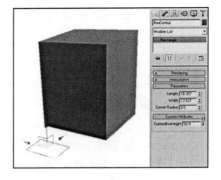

## EXPRESSIONS

An *expression* is a short equation that you can use to customize the effect one parameter has on another.

For example, suppose you want to the box's actual height to be half the value of the CustomBoxHeight parameter. In other words, when CustomBoxHeight is 50, you want the box's height to be 25. You could use an expression similar to the following:

**Box's height = CustomBoxHeight / 2**

You can enter an expression like this right in the Parameter Wiring dialog. The entry areas at the bottom of the dialog are there just for this purpose.

Let's try out this expression on the practice scene.

> ### ☀ TIP ☀
>
> *You can use a variety of symbols in expressions. The most common ones are:*
>
> | | |
> |---|---|
> | + Add | - Subtract |
> | * Multiply | / Divide |
> | < Less than | > Greater than |

In this practice exercise, you will learn to use expressions with wiring.

**Change the Box Height Expression**

1. Load the file *Practice_CA01.max* that you created earlier, or load this file from the *Practice* folder on the CD.

2. Select **BoxControl**, the rectangle.

3. Choose *Animation menu* > *Wire Parameters* > *Parameter Wire Dialog* to open the Parameter Wiring dialog.

4. Expand the listing on the left to show **BoxControl** > **Object (Rectangle)** > **Custom Attributes** > **CustomBoxHeight**.

5. Highlight the **CustomBoxHeight** listing.

6. On the right side of the dialog, above the listings, click the **Find next parameter** button.

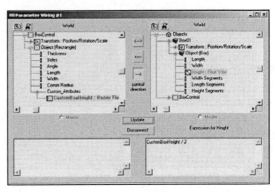

The **Find next parameter** button finds wired parameters in the dialog. If you click it once, the listing on the right will jump to the parameter wired to the **CustomBoxHeight** listing, which is the box's **Height** parameter on the right. You can confirm that it's the correct parameter by looking at the right arrow button. This button is turned on to show that the highlighted parameters are wired together, and that the one on the left controls the one on the right.

Below the listing on the right is an entry area with the text **CustomBoxHeight**. This is the expression currently being used to define the box's **Height** parameter.

7. In the entry area on the right side of the dialog, enter **/ 2** after **CustomBoxHeight**.

8. Click **Update**.

This updates the wiring to use the new expression.

You can test the new expression by changing the **CustomBoxHeight** parameter on the **Modify** panel. The box's height should always be half the **CustomBoxHeight** value.

9. Close the Parameter Wiring dialog.

### Create a Rotation Attribute

In character rigging, you will frequently wire custom attributes and controls to the rotation of bones and IK chains. Wiring rotation parameters often requires the use of a special expression. Let's see what happens when you wire the box's rotation on its X axis to a custom attribute.

1. Select **BoxControl**, and choose *Animation menu > Add Custom Attribute*.

2. On the Add Parameter dialog, enter **CustomXRotation** for the **Name**, and enter a **Range** from **0** to **360**. Click **Add** to add the custom attribute, and close the dialog.

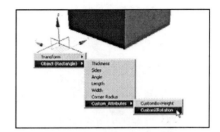

### Wire the Rotation Attribute

Now you're ready to wire the parameter. To make it easier, you'll use an alternate method of choosing the parameters to wire.

1. With **BoxControl** selected, choose *Animation menu > Wire Parameters > Wire Parameters*.

   A pop-up menu appears over the **BoxControl** object, showing the possible selections for the next level of listings.

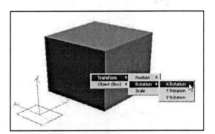

2. From the pop-up menu, choose *Object (Rectangle) > Custom Attributes > CustomXRotation*.

3. Move the cursor to the box. A dotted line appears from the rectangle to the box. Click the box.

4. On the pop-up menu that appears, choose *Transform > Rotation > X Rotation*.

   The Parameter Wiring dialog appears, with the correct parameters already selected on each side of the dialog.

5. Click the right arrow button, and click **Connect**.

6. Minimize the dialog by clicking the **[–]** at the upper right corner of the dialog.

7. On the **Modify** panel, change the **CustomXRotation** value to rotate the box.

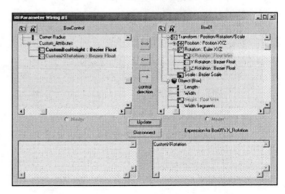

The box spins wildly even if you increase **CustomXRotation** by just a small amount. This is because, by default, 3ds max calculates rotation values in *radians*. Like degrees, a radian is a unit used for measuring angles. One radian is equal to about 57 degrees.

## Use a Function to Convert to Radians

To make the custom attribute work more intuitively, you can write an expression to convert the **CustomXRotation** value to radians before passing it on to the box's X rotation. You could simply divide **CustomXRotation** by 57, but this wouldn't be perfectly accurate. Instead, you'll use a function to make the conversion.

A *function* is a command you can use in an expression to perform a specific mathematical operation. 3ds max has many built-in functions. Here, you will use a function called **degtorad** which converts a number from degrees to radians. The result is the same as dividing the number by 57.29598, the number of degrees in a radian.

Here, you'll use the **degtorad** function to convert the slider value to radians before passing it on to the box's X-axis rotation.

1. Click the Parameter Wiring dialog at the lower left corner of the screen to open it.

   **Note:** If you closed the dialog rather than minimized it, you can open it again using *Animation menu > Wire Parameters > Parameter Wire Dialog*. However, you will have to expand the listings again and highlight them before continuing.

2. In the entry area at the lower right of the dialog, replace **CustomXRotation** with **degtorad(CustomXRotation)**.

   Putting the **CustomXRotation** in parentheses converts **CustomXRotation** to radians before passing it on to the box's X rotation.

3. Click **Update**.

4. Close the Parameter Wiring dialog.

5. Increase **CustomXRotation** and observe the result.

   The rotation now works more intuitively, increasing the rotation by the number of degrees set by **CustomXRotation**.

6. Save the scene as **Practice_CA02.max**.

> ## ☃ TIP ☃
>
> *To understand what a radian is, try the following:*
>
> *Create a polygon from two radii on a circle, and the arc between them. When the length of the arc is equal to the radius, the angle between the two radii is one radian. A full circle has 2 * pi radians.*

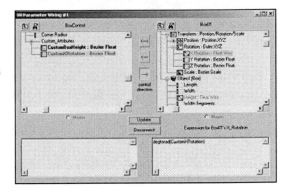

This is the fun part, where you start creating controls for your character rig. Using the tools you've just learned, you'll create custom attributes so you can roll the character's feet with parameters on the **Modify** panel.

**Load the Character**

1. Load the file *CharRig07.max* that you created earlier, or load it from the *Rigs* folder on the CD.

   Recall that you have already added several IK chains to the character's legs and feet, and that you've linked them together. Let's review the object names.

2. Select a few of the IK chains, and look at the name of each one on the Modify panel. You can select an IK chain by clicking on the crosshairs for each one. This will refresh your memory as to how they're named.

3. If you've forgotten how the IK chains work, move or rotate a few of them, then undo what you've done. In particular, recall that you rotate the heel upward by rotating **IKBallL** or **IKBallR** on its local X axis.

**Create Control Objects**

To simplify the process of animating your character, you'll create a control object for each foot, and add all the foot-related custom attributes to these objects.

1. In the Top viewport, zoom out a little to make room to place the control objects.

2. In the Top viewport, create a rectangle a little larger than one of the feet. Name the rectangle **CtrlFootL**.

   If you like, you can increase the rectangle's **Corner Radius** parameter to give it rounded edges.

3. If necessary, move the rectangle so it sits just under the left foot.

4. Create a copy of the rectangle, and name it **CtrlFootR**. Place this object under the right foot.

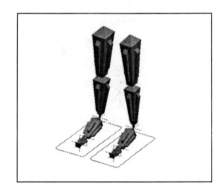

## Link the Overall Foot Controls

1. Select **IKToeL** (the IK chain at the tip of the left foot), and link it to **CtrlFootL**.

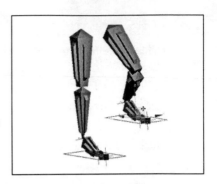

2. To test the rig, go to frame 10, turn on **Auto Key**, and move **CtrlFootL** upward and to the side.

   The entire foot moves with it, as you would expect, but there's a problem. The foot bone spins when you move the foot. You can keep it from spinning by adjusting one of the controls for the IK chain at the ball of the foot.

3. Turn off **Auto Key**.

4. Select **IKBallL**, the IK chain at the ball of the left foot, and go to the **Motion** panel.

   Locate the IK Solver Properties rollout. You can keep the bones from spinning by changing the *parent space*, or reference point, that the IK chain uses. Right now, it's set to use the **Start Joint** as a reference point, which is at the ankle in this case. Because the ankle changes its rotation when you move **CtrlFootL** up and down, the bones swivel. To solve this problem, you'll use the **IK Goal** setting to keep the bones from spinning when you move **CtrlFootL**.

   If you've changed the **Swivel Angle**, reset it to **0** before continuing.

5. In the Parent Space group, select the **IK Goal** option.

   If this causes the bone to turn on its side, change the **Swivel Angle** to **-90** or **90** to correct it.

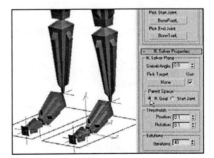

6. Select **IKToeL**, and set its parent space to **IK Goal**. Change the **Swivel Angle** if necessary.

   This will avoid problems in the future with later parts of the rig causing the bones to spin.

7. Move the time slider to see the foot rise. The bones don't rotate this time.

8. Perform the same tasks on the right foot. Test the rig by animating **CtrlFootR** on frame 10. Check that the foot moves with the control object, and that the bones don't rotate independently of the foot control.

   Be sure to turn off **Auto Key** when you have finished.

### ☀ TIP ☀

*It's fine to animate the rig before applying the Skin modifier, as long as you don't change the rig on frame 0.*

---

## Add Custom Attributes

Now you can add custom attributes to control the feet. You'll start with a custom attribute for rolling the left foot. A range of 0 to 90 degrees will work well for this custom attribute.

1. Select **CtrlFootL**.

2. Choose *Animation menu > Add Custom Attribute*. The Add Parameter dialog appears.

3. For **Name**, enter **Roll**.

4. On the Float UI Options rollout, change the **Range** to go from **0** to **90**.

5. On the Finish rollout, click **Add**.

   You can see the new parameter on the **Modify** panel, on the Custom Attributes rollout. You don't have to close the Add Parameters dialog to add the custom attribute to the other foot control.

6. Select **CtrlFootR**, and enter **Roll** as the **Name** on the Add Parameters dialog. Click **Add** to add the custom attribute to the right foot control.

7. Close the Add Parameters dialog.

## Wire the Left Foot Roll

Now you will wire the **Roll** parameter to cause the heel to come off the ground. Before setting up the wiring, you should increase the active time segment. By default, parameter wiring works only over the time segment that was active when you set up the wiring. Although you can change this in Track View after setting up the wiring, it's usually easier to set the time segment to the longest time you think you'll need before doing the wiring.

1. Click **Time Configuration**, and set the **Length** of the animation to **10000**. Click **OK** to close the dialog.

2. Select **CtrlFootL**.

3. Choose *Animation menu > Wire Parameters > Wire Parameters*.

4. From the pop-up menu, choose *Object (Rectangle) > Custom Attributes > Roll*.

5. Click **IKBallL**, and choose *Transform > IK Goal > Rotation > X Rotation* from the pop-up menu. The Parameter Wiring dialog appears.

6. In the lower right entry area, change **Roll** to **degtorad(Roll)**.

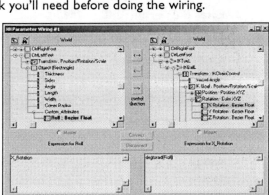

7. Click the right arrow button in the middle of the dialog, and click **Connect**.

   If the Parameter Wiring dialog is in the way of your seeing the leg rig, you can move it aside for now.

8. Select **CtrlFootL** and access the **Modify** panel. Change the **Roll** parameter, and observe the result.

   If all has gone well, the heel should rise as you increase the parameter. If it doesn't work, look back over this tutorial to see where you might have gone wrong. If you still can't get it to work, start the tutorial over again.

   The foot bone might flip or spin when **Roll** reaches 70 or 80. By the time you complete the rig, this problem will be solved.

9. Close the Parameter Wiring dialog.

## Wire the Right Foot Roll

Now you will use the procedure you just learned to wire the right foot.

1. Select **CtrlFootR**, and choose *Animation menu > Wire Parameters > Wire Parameters*. From the pop-up menu, choose *Object (Rectangle) > Custom Attributes > Roll*.

2. Select **IKBallR**, and choose *Transform > IK Goal > Rotation > X Rotation* from the pop-up menu.

3. Enter **degtorad(Roll)** in the lower right entry area.

4. Click the right arrow button in the middle of the dialog, and click **Connect**.

5. Close the Parameter Wiring dialog.

6. Test the wiring by increasing the **Roll** parameter for **CtrlFootR**. If the right heel raises off the ground, you've got it right.

7. Reset the **Roll** values to **0** before continuing.

   Resetting the **Roll** values to 0 isn't strictly necessary, but it make it easier for you to figure out what's going on when you wire the parameters in later steps.

8. Save the scene as **CharRig08.max**.

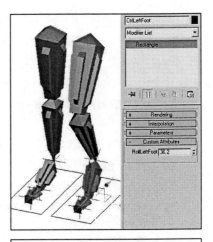

Right now, when you change the **Roll** parameter, the heel comes off the ground. But what about the toe? Eventually, the toe will have to rotate so the entire foot can come off the ground.

You can make the **Roll** parameter affect the rotation of the toe as well as the ball of the foot. Any wired parameter can affect more than one parameter in the scene. This type of multiple wiring is very handy for controlling more than one part of the character with a single control.

In this case, you're going to have the **Roll** parameter affect the toe rotation, but only when **Roll** exceeds 35 degrees. The expression you will use for the IK chain at the toe, in plain English, will follow this logic:

**If Roll < 35, do nothing.**
**Otherwise, start rotating.**

If you didn't complete the previous tutorial, you can load *CharRig08.max* from the *Rigs* folder on the CD to do this tutorial.

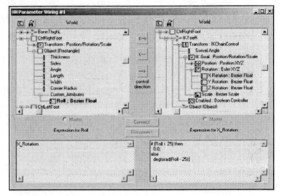

1. Select **CtrlFootR**. Choose *Animation menu > Wire Parameters > Wire Parameters*. From the pop-up menu, choose *Object (Rectangle) > Custom Attributes > Roll*.

2. Select **IKToeR**, and choose *Transform > IK Goal > Rotation > X Rotation* from the pop-up menu.

3. in the lower right entry area, replace the existing text with the following expression:

```
if (Roll < 35) then
   0.0;
else
   degtorad(Roll - 35);
```

This expression is a little like programming, using **if** and **else** to set conditions for different values for **IKToeR**. This expression says that if **Roll** is under 35, **IKToeR** should not rotate. If **Roll** goes over 35, **IKToeR** should start to rotate by **Roll** minus 35. For example, if **Roll** is 42, **IKToeR** will rotate by 7 degrees, raising the toe slightly off the ground.

4. Click the right arrow, and click **Connect**.

5. Select **CtrlFootR**, and change the **Roll** parameter to see if it works. The toe should start to come off the ground after **Roll** reaches 35 degrees.

   If the toe doesn't rise as expected when **Roll** exceeds 35, check the expression in the Parameter Wiring dialog to make sure it's correct. If you make corrections, click **Update** to see the effect of the changes.

6. Use the same process to wire the toe roll for the **CtrlFootL**, wiring its **Roll** parameter to **IKToeL** > *Transform* > *IK Goal* > *Rotation* > *X Rotation*.

7. Close the Parameter Wiring dialog.

8. Save the scene as **CharRig09.max**.

### Reduce the Ball Roll

When you increase **Roll** past 35 degrees, the heel continues to rise. This does not represent natural movement. In life, when you bring your foot off the ground, it starts to straighten after the toe comes up. By the time the toe reaches a 90-degree angle with the ground, the foot is nearly or completely straight.

With the rig the way it is now, the heel rotates doubly after the toe starts to come off the ground—once from the IK chain at the ball, and once from the IK chain at the toe. So instead of straightening after the toe starts to come off the ground, the foot bends even more. This will make your character look as though he's about to get a very bad cramp in his foot.

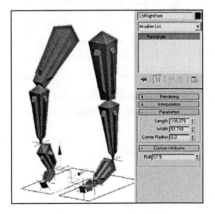

We can fix this with a more detailed expression for **IKBallL** and **IKBallR**. Basically, we'll say that when **Roll** reaches 35, the ball should start rotating the other way to straighten the foot.

Since wiring already exists for each of the ball IK chains, there's a quick way to get the wired parameters to appear in the Parameter Wiring dialog.

1. Select **IKBallL**.

2. Right-click the trackbar at the bottom of the screen, and choose *Controller Properties* > *IKBallL: X Rotation* from the pop-up menu.

   The Parameter Wiring dialog appears, but the wiring expression is on the left rather than the right.

In the entry area at the bottom left of the dialog, replace **degtorad(Roll)** with the following expression:

```
if (Roll < 35) then
  degtorad(Roll);
else
  degtorad(70-Roll);
```

This expression is a little more complicated. Basically, we needed to find a way to gradually reduce the ball's rotation as **Roll** passes 35 and gets larger.

Let's look at how this works. Suppose **Roll** is larger than 35, which means the expression **degtorad(70-Roll)** will be used. This equation causes the X rotation for **IKBallL** to decrease as **Roll** increases beyond 35. I used the number 70 because it's equal to 2 times 35, so the change from increasing to decreasing rotation will be smooth when **Roll** reaches 35.

To come up with this expression, I had to get out a piece of paper and mess around with the numbers, then I tried a few different expressions before hitting on one that created the result I wanted.

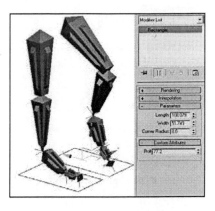

 3. On the Parameter Wiring dialog, click **Update**.

 4. Test the new expression by changing **Roll** on the **Modify** panel. The heel should rise, then the toe should start rising when **Roll** passes 35. The foot should straighten out by the time **Roll** reaches about **90**.

Also note that the foot no longer flips or spins when **Roll** reaches **70** or **80**. The IK solvers at each joint in the foot give you complete control over what the foot is doing.

5. Do the same process on the right foot. changing the wiring expression for **IKBallR**.

6. Test the wiring by increasing the **Roll** value for the right foot control.

7. Before saving, set both **Roll** parameters to **0.0**.

You now have several ways to control the feet. You can move or rotate a control object to animate the entire foot, and you can make the foot roll by animating the **Roll** value.

8. Save the scene as **CharRig10.max**.

☙ TIP ☙

*Have you ever sat in math class and wondered, "What the heck am I ever going to use this for?" Well, now you know.*

## RIG CONTROLS

Now that the legs have been rigged, you need some controls for twisting and bending the spine, and for controlling the arms and head. For this, you'll use a few custom shapes. The image at right shows the final result.

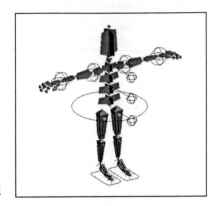

Why are we using shapes to control the character? Shapes don't render, so you can leave the shapes onscreen when you render the animation. In addition, they don't use up as much memory as geometry. This becomes important when you have many characters or objects in a scene. The less memory each character uses up, the faster the screen will refresh.

If you wanted to, you could use helper objects such as Point or Dummy objects to control the character. Like shapes, these objects don't render and use little memory. But for our rig, we'll use shapes only. This will allow us to use the *selection filter* during the animation process. The selection filter limits your selection possibilities to one type of object, such as shapes. You'll find out how to use the selection filter in the *Character Animation* chapter.

## WHAT SHOULD THE SHAPES CONTROL?

When setting up a character rig, you will always be concerned with what types of motion the character will be able to do with the rig. There goal here is to use a few simple controls that give you the ability to pose the character in a variety of ways.

To break down the controls, let's take a look at the spine first. What kinds of motions can you make with your own spine? If your back, shoulders and neck are in good health, you can:

- Bend forward or backward, or from side to side

- Twist at the shoulders while keeping your hips straight

- Twist at the hips to turn your entire spine

- Shake, nod, or tilt your head independently of your shoulders and spine

Setting up a rig that accommodates all these poses requires a little ingenuity. You won't need IK for the spine; FK will do the trick.

You'll need at least two controls on the spine, and one for the neck and head. Unless you want to put a control at each joint, you'll also have to get clever with your linking and wiring. I'll show you how to do this in the exercises that follow.

## PIVOT POINTS

In order to continue with the rigging process, you'll need to get a thorough grasp of another important animation concept: *pivot points*. An object's pivot point sets the orientation for the local XYZ axes, which determine which way the object rotates on any given axis.

When you create an object, bone, shape, or any other type of object in 3ds max, the pivot point and local axes are placed automatically. For bones, the pivot point is placed where you clicked when you started creating the bone, which is the spot between the bone and its parent. For example, the calf bone's pivot point is at the knee, where the thigh and calf bones meet.

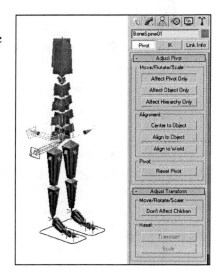

For other objects, 3ds max usually places the pivot point at the center of the object. When you transform an object (move, rotate, scale), the transform gizmo appears at the object's pivot point, and the object transforms in relationship to that point.

When you link one object to another then rotate the parent object, the child rotates around the parent's pivot point. You have already seen this when you linked two IK chains together on the foot. When you rotated the parent IK chain, the child rotated around the parent.

This fact will also come into play when you set up the spine rig. If you want the spine to rotate along with the control shapes, you will have to work with pivot points.

You can change an object's pivot point on the Hierarchy panel. Select the object, click Affect Pivot Only, and move or rotate the pivot point.

 You can also use the Align tool when Affect Pivot Only is turned on. This is a very efficient way to align one object's pivot point to another's. You'll use this technique often when you rig the spine.

## CUSTOM SHAPES

There are many custom shapes you can use to rig a character. You have already set up rectangles to control the feet. For the rest of the body, you'll use the following shapes as controls for specific body parts:

- **Gyro** - A shape made of three circles. It's used for joints that rotate around all three axes, such as wrists and shoulders.

- **Gyrohandle** - An alternate version of the gyro that includes a handle. This shape is used to control joints in larger areas of the body, such as the spine. The handle makes the shape easier to select and animate.

- **Circle** - A plain old circle. Two or more other controls are linked to it, such as the leg and spine controls.

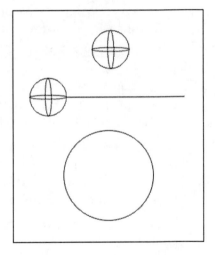

For the gyrohandle, the pivot point is at the tip of the handle. This means that when you rotate the gyrohandle, the object will rotate around its tip.

For the gyro, the pivot point can be at its center or elsewhere, depending on what's required for that part of the rig.

For the circle, the pivot point is always at the center of the shape.

You will use gyrohandles to control the spine. You can create your own shapes, or use the ones provided on the CD.

### Merge the First Spine Control

1. Load the file *CharRig10.max* that you created earlier, or load this file from the *Rigs* folder on the CD.

2. Unhide the spine bones **BoneSpine01** through **BoneSpine04**.

3. Click **Zoom Extents All** so you can see the legs and spine.

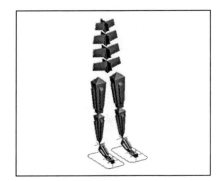

4. To merge the gyrohandle shape for the scene, choose *File menu > Merge*. Select the file *ControlShapes.max* from the *Rigs* folder on the CD, and select the object **GyroHandle**.

   If you choose to create this shape yourself, be sure to place the control object's pivot point at the end of the straight portion of the handle.

5. Name the gyrohandle **CtrlSpineBase**. You will use this control shape to rotate the entire spine.

### Align and Link the Spine Control

1. Use **Align** to align the control shape to the lowest spine bone. In the Align dialog, turn on **Pivot Point** for both the Current Object and Target Object.

2. Rotate the control object so it sticks out in front of the character.

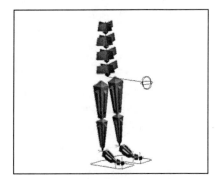

   The gyrohandle will control the entire spine. Since the spine is already linked together, the only thing you need to do to get a basic spine rig is link the bottom spine bone to the control object.

3. Link **BoneSpine01** to **CtrlSpineBase**.

4. Test the setup by rotating **CtrlSpineBase** on any axis.

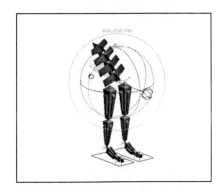

   The object rotates from its pivot point, which is positioned at the bottom of the spine. This causes the entire spine to rotate in the same direction you rotated the control shape. Undo any rotation before continuing.

5. Save the scene as **CharRig11.max**.

### Set up Double Rotation

When you twist your spine, the bones at the top of your spine tend to rotate more than those at the bottom. You can make the rig do the same thing automatically by using wiring.

Here, you will wire the rotation of the second-lowest spine bone to the control shape. In this way, when you rotate the control shape, the bone will receive the rotation twice: Once for the wiring, and once as a child of the bottom spine bone. As a result, the second-lowest spine bone will rotate twice as much as the lowest one when you rotate the control shape.

This will simulate the natural rotation of the spine, where the upper bones rotate more than the lower bones.

1. Select **CtrlSpineBase**.

2. Choose *Animation menu > Wire Parameters > Wire Parameters,* and choose *Transform > Rotation > X Rotation* from the pop-up menu. Click **BoneSpine02** and choose *Transform > Rotation > X Rotation* from the pop-up menu.

   Because you'll be wiring every axis of the control shape to every axis of the bone, you can save time by wiring the entire **Rotation** listing.

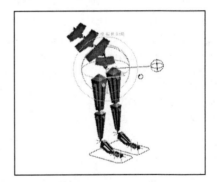

3. On the Parameter Wiring dialog, select the **Rotation** listing on each side (the one above X Rotation).

4. Click the right arrow and **Connect** to make the Rotation listing on the left control the one on the right, and close the Parameter Wiring dialog.

   Woops! The wired spine bone turns in the wrong direction, taking the rest of the spine with it. In addition, if you rotate the control shape, the spine rotates in all kinds of strange directions that have nothing to do with the control shape's rotation. Something's definitely wrong here.

   Why isn't it working? One of the problems is that the control object, and perhaps the spine, have been rotated at one time or another to put them in their current places. The wiring is adding up all the control shape's rotations on whatever its local axes are, and affecting the bone's local axes with this rotation. The chances of this resulting in the expected rotation is pretty slim.

You don't get this problem with linking, which is why the bottom spine bone worked fine when you linked it to the control shape. With linking, the child object always follows the parent object's current orientation. This problem is strictly a wiring phenomenon. However, there's no way to get the double rotation effect with linking alone--you'll have to use wiring for this effect.

You'll get the same result even if you wire individual rotation parameters to one another. For example, wiring the X Rotation of the control shape to the bone's X Rotation parameter won't give you the expected rotation either. You might be able to get some success by doing some cross-wiring, such as wiring the control shape's Z Rotation to the bone's X Rotation, or some variation of this. But you could drive yourself crazy trying to figure out the correct wiring, which might require putting in negative signs and subtracting from 90 or 180 or whatever. Not a fun way to spend your time, and there's an easier way.

To figure out how to solve this problem, let's examine it more closely. There are three situations to address before the wiring will work properly:

> **☆ TIP ☆**
>
> *There's no need to save the scene again since you'll be starting from the last saved file, CharRig11.max, when you correct this problem.*

- You want the control shape's local axes to match the bone's, so any rotation on the control shape will rotate the bone on the same axis. You can solve this problem by aligning the control shape's pivot point to the bone's pivot point. This is an easy task that you can perform with the **Align** tool.

- If the spine bone was rotated to pose it in place, it had an original orientation when it was created, and now it has its current orientation. You want the spine bone to be affected in relationship to its current orientation, not its original orientation.

- The same goes for the control shape. You want to control the spine with changes to the control shape's current orientation, not its original orientation.

The second and third problems require a little more work. You'll need to use a *controller* to hold two different sets of information for the spine bone and control object: The change from the original orientation to the current orientation, and any additional rotation beyond that. Then you can make the wiring affect only the additional rotation.

So what's a controller? Read on to find out.

# CONTROLLERS

A *controller* is an alternate method for specifying an object's transforms (position, rotation, and scale). For example, you could define an object's position with a Path controller, which will cause the object to follow a specific shape (path) in the scene. You could also define an object's rotation with a LookAt controller, which will force one of the object's axes to always "look at" another object in the scene.

By default, a simple controller is assigned to each of an object's three transforms. If you just went ahead and animated the objects in the scene, you might never know the controllers were there. 3ds max provides additional controllers so you'll have more flexibility when animating.

## ☙ TIP ☙

*In the 3ds max documentation, controllers are also called "animation controllers" or "constraints".*

In effect, controllers determine the types of parameters that will be available when you animate. Although you can do a lot with a scene with simple parameter wiring, controllers can provide much more sweeping effects on an object's transforms.

You assign controllers on the Motion panel, on the Assign Controller rollout. Highlight the controller you want to change, then click the Assign Controller button. Choose the controller from the list that appears.

## LIST CONTROLLERS

A *list controller* allows you to use two or more controllers at once for the same transform. The controllers are evaluated from first to last, so you can use the first one to hold an offset in position or rotation from an object's original transforms.

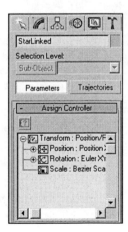

In the situation involving the spine, you'll use a list controller to hold the change from the original orientation to the current rotation, and another controller for the animated rotation.

If list controllers don't make sense to you, do the practice exercise to get a better grasp of how they work. Then you'll be able to use them on the character rig.

## Practice N: Using List Controllers

Here, you will use controllers on a simple practice scene. You can use the technique you learn in this exercise to rig the double rotation in the next tutorial.

### Load the Practice Scene

1. Load the file *Practice_ListController01.max* from the *Rigs* folder on the CD.

   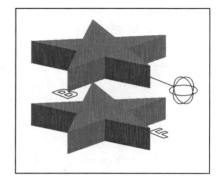

   This file contains two star objects and a gyrohandle just like the one you are using to control the character's spine. The topmost star, **StarBase**, is linked to the handle, and the lower star, **StarLinked**, is linked to **StarBase**. The F and B designations are linked to the lower star object to help you keep track of the star's front and back.

2. Rotate the gyrohandle to rotate both stars.

   So far, everything works as expected. Let's do it another way, by using wiring to make the gyrohandle rotate the star.

### Attempt to Wire the Rotation

1. Select the gyrohandle.

2. Choose *Animation menu > Wire Parameters > Wire Parameters*, and choose *Transform > Rotation > X Rotation* from the pop-up menu. Click **StarLinked**, the lower star, and choose *Transform > Rotation > X Rotation* from the pop-up menu.

3. On the Parameter Wiring dialog, select the **Rotation** listing on each side (the one above X Rotation).

4. Click the right arrow and **Connect** to make the Rotation listing on the left control the one on the right.

   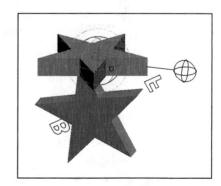

5. Rotate the gyrohandle. Recall that it will rotate from the center of the top star, where its pivot point is located.

   Here, you see the same phenomenon you saw on the wiring between the control shape and the bone. The lower star spins in various directions that have nothing to do with the rotation of the gyrohandle.

6. Undo the rotation and wiring, or reload *Practice_ListController01.max*.

### Align the Pivot Points

Ideally, you want a control object's pivot point's orientation to match the object it will control. That way, when you rotate the control object around a specific axis, the object it's wired to will rotate around the same axis, making animation with the rig very intuitive.

One of the pivot points will have to be adjusted to match the other. The most sensible solution is to change the control object's pivot point to match the object it's controlling.

This procedure is a little different from the alignment operation you did in the last tutorial. There, you moved the *control shape* to align its pivot with the spine. Now you are going to rotate the *pivot point* without visibly affecting the control shape.

1. Select the gyrohandle.

2. On the **Hierarchy** panel, click **Affect Pivot Only**.

3. Click **Align**, and click the lower star. In the Align Orientation group, turn on **X**, **Y** and **Z**.

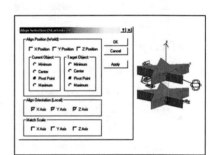

   As you turn on each axis, you will see the pivot point change its orientation in viewports.

4. Click **OK** to set the alignment.

5. Turn off **Affect Pivot Only**.

   You might think that would be enough to make the wiring work, but it's not. You still have the issue of the initial orientation vs. The current orientation to contend with. We'll use controllers to make it work.

### Inspect the Current Controllers

Let's take a look at the controllers that are currently set up for the gyrohandle and the lower star.

1. Select **StarLinked**, the lower star.

2. Go to the **Motion** panel.

3. On the **Motion** panel, expand the Assign Controller rollout.

The Assign Controller rollout shows the controllers currently assigned to the three transforms: Position, Rotation and Scale. The Rotation controller is currently set to Euler XYZ, the default rotation controller for all 3ds max objects.

4. Click the **[+]** next to the Rotation listing to expand it.

Here you can see the three parameters that have always been available to you for wiring: X Rotation, Y Rotation and Z Rotation.

This Euler XYZ controller currently holds any rotation already done on the star, which represents the posed orientation. What we want to do is set up another Euler XYZ controllers after the current one, which will control the animated rotation.

5. Click the **[-]** next to the Rotation listing to collapse the listing.

**Set up the New Controller**

1. Highlight the **Rotation** listing on the Assign Controller rollout.

2. Click the **Assign Controller** button at the top of the Assign Controller rollout.

3. On the Assign Rotation Controller dialog, highlight **Rotation List** and click **OK**.

4. On the Assign Controller dialog, click the **[+]** next to Rotation to expand the listing. Scroll the listing to see all the new listings under Rotation.

The Rotation List controller is a type of list controller. It creates a list where you can assign as many rotation controllers as you like. The Euler XYZ controller has been pushed down to the first controller on the list, and still holds the object's posed orientation. The next listing is called Available, then the next is Weights.

The Available listing is a placeholder for the next controller you want to assign. We want another Euler XYZ controller, so let's assign it.

5. Highlight the **Available** listing.

6. Click the **Assign Controller** button, and choose **Euler XYZ**.

☀ **TIP** ☀

*The Euler XYZ controller is named after Leonhard Euler, an 18th-century Swiss mathematician who came up with new ways to work with angles of rotation.*

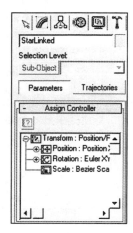

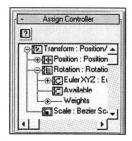

Now you have two **Euler XYZ** controllers, followed by an **Available** listing in case we want to assign another controller (which we don't).

At any given time, only one controller is active. By default, the first controller is active. We want the second controller to be active so when we animate the object, the second controller will be used.

You can set the active controller on the Rotation List rollout. There, you can see the two **Euler XYZ** controllers listed. The first has a small arrow in front of it to indicate it is active.

To make the process of picking controllers easier, you'll change their names.

### Set the Active Controller

1. In the Rotation List rollout, highlight the first **Euler XYZ** controller, the one preceded by the small arrow.

2. In the Rotation List rollout, place the cursor in the entry box just below the two Euler XYZ listings. Enter the name **Pose**.

   This name indicates that the controller sets the currently posed orientation for the object. The new name appears in the listing above the entry area.

3. Highlight the second Euler XYZ listing on the Rotation List rollout, and enter the name **Animation**.

   This name indicates that this controller will be used to animate the object.

4. In the Rotation List rollout, double-click the **Animation** listing until the small arrow appears in front of it.

   Now the Animation controller is the active controller.

   Next, you must do the same for the gyrohandle so it has a Rotation List controller as well.

5. Perform the two previous procedures on the gyroshape, naming the two controllers **Pose** and **Animation** as you did for the star. Make sure the **Animation** controller is the active controller before continuing.

## Wire the Rotation

Now you can wire the two **Animation** controllers together. The **Animation** controllers currently have rotation values of 0,0,0 and start from the objects' pivot points. In terms of rotation, each **Animation** controller will pick up where its corresponding **Pose** controller left off, so there will be no conflict between the posed and animation rotation. This means you can just wire the two **Animation** controllers together and be done with it.

1. Select the gyrohandle.

   When you do the wiring this time around, there will be some new options on the pop-up menu. When you choose *Transform > Rotation*, you will see the new controllers.

2. Choose *Animation menu > Wire Parameters > Wire Parameters,* and choose *Transform > Rotation > Animation > X Rotation* from the pop-up menu. Click **StarLinked**, and choose *Transform > Rotation > Animation > X Rotation* from the pop-up menu.

3. On the Parameter Wiring dialog, highlight the **Animation** listing on each side.

4. Click the right arrow and **Connect** to make the Animation listing on the left control the one on the right.

5. Rotate the gyrohandle.

   Magic! The lower star now rotates in the same direction as both the gyrohandle and the upper star. It receives double the rotation due to the linking plus the wiring.

   This is the effect we were trying to achieve with the spine bones. You will use this same technique to create double-rotation wiring on the spine.

6. Save the scene as **Practice_ListController02.max**.

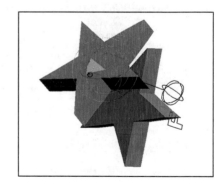

Now you can use what you've learned about list controllers to finish setting up the spine rig.

### Align the Control Shape's Pivot Point

As always, the first order of business is to align the pivot points of the two objects you want to control with the wiring. Doing this before you create the list controller ensures that the current orientation will be part of the existing Euler XYZ controller, which will become the Pose controller in the next procedure.

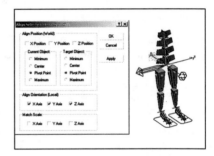

1. Load the file *CharRig11.max* that you created earlier, or load this file from the *Rigs* folder on the CD.

2. Select **CtrlSpineBase**, the gyrohandle that controls the spine.

3. On the **Hierarchy** panel, click **Affect Pivot Only**.

4. Click **Align**, and click **BoneSpine02**, the second-lowest spine bone.

5. In the Align dialog, do not change the Align Position. In the Align Orientation group, turn on **X, Y** and **Z**. Make sure **Pivot Point** is selected for both Current Object and Target Object, and click **OK**.

6. Turn off **Affect Pivot Only**.

### Set up the Rotation Controllers

Now you can get on to solving the bigger problem of the original versus current orientation. To solve this problem, you will set up a list controller for both the control shape and the second-lowest spine bone.

1. With **CtrlSpineBase** still selected, go to the **Motion** panel.

2. Highlight the **Rotation** listing in the Assign Controller rollout, click the **Assign Controller** button, and assign a **Rotation List** controller.

3. Expand the **Rotation** listing on the Assign Controller rollout. Highlight **Available**, and assign a second **Euler XYZ** controller.

4. On the Rotation List rollout, name the controllers **Pose** and **Animation**, respectively.

5. If necessary, double-click the **Animation** controller on the Rotation List rollout to make the arrow appear in front of it, which makes it the current controller.

6. Do the same procedure to set up a Rotation List controller for **BoneSpine02**, the second-lowest spine bone. Double-click the **Animation** controller to make it the current controller.

☺ **TIP** ☺

Since you won't be doing any wiring with the lowest spine bone, there is no need to assign a list controller to it.

## Wire the Rotation

1. Select **CtrlSpineBase**.

2. Right-click **CtrlSpineBase**, and choose *Wire Parameters* from the Quad menu. Choose *Transform > Rotation > Animation > X Rotation* from the pop-up menu. Click **BoneSpine02**, and choose *Transform > Rotation > Animation > X Rotation* from the pop-up menu.

☺ **TIP** ☺

Choosing Wire Parameters from the Quad menu is another way to start the wiring process.

You could wire each of the rotation listings to one another (X Rotation, Y Rotation, Z Rotation), but you can save time by wiring the **Animation** listings together. This automatically wires each of the X, Y and Z rotation listings to one another.

3. On the Parameter Wiring dialog, highlight the **Animation : Euler XYZ** listing on each side (the one above X Rotation).

4. Click the right arrow, then click **Connect**.

5. Close the Parameter Wiring dialog.

6. Test the wiring by rotating **CtrlSpineBase**. The second spine bone from the bottom should rotate twice as much as the bottom spine bone when you rotate the gyrohandle in any direction. Undo any rotation before continuing.

7. Save the scene as **CharRig12.max**.

## Create the Remaining Spine Controls

The rig for the upper spine and neck works similarly to the rig at the bottom of the spine. Now you know all the tricks, so it's just a matter of setting it up.

1. Unhide **BoneNeck** and **BoneHead**.

2. Create two copies of **CtrlSpineBase**, and name them **CtrlSpineMid** and **CtrlSpineNeck**.

First, you will align the positions of these new controls to the bones that will link to them.

3. Use **Align** to align the position and orientation of **CtrlSpineNeck** with **BoneNeck**. Set both Current Object and Target Object to **Pivot Point** on the Align dialog.

4. Align **CtrlSpineMid** with **BoneSpine03** (the second spine bone from the top), aligning both the position and orientation.

Now you can link the bones to the controls.

5. Link **BoneNeck** to **CtrlSpineNeck**.

6. Link **BoneSpine03** to **CtrlSpineMid**.

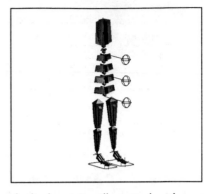

### Align the Pivot Points

Next, you will change the orientation of each control object's pivot point to match the bone it will control with wiring. The pivot point orientations for all the bones are similar, but to be safe, you should align the pivot points for each set of controls and bones.

Recall that you aligned the control object pivot point's *position* with the bone that will be linked to it, but you align the pivot point's *orientation* to the bone that will receive the double rotation.

1. Select **CtrlSpineNeck**.

2. On the **Hierarchy** panel, turn on **Affect Pivot Only**.

3. Align the orientation of **CtrlSpineNeck**'s pivot point to **BoneHead**'s pivot point.

4. Select **CtrlSpineMid**, and align the orientation of **CtrlSpineMid**'s pivot point to **BoneSpine04**'s pivot point.

Be sure to turn off **Affect Pivot Only** before continuing.

> ### ☙ TIP ☙
> You can leave *Affect Pivot Only* turned on while you select other objects and work with their pivot points.

### Wire the Neck and Upper Spine

1. In the same way you did earlier, set up Rotation List controllers for **BoneHead** and **BoneSpine04**. Name the two controllers **Pose** and **Animation** for each object, and set the current controller to **Animation**.

2. Wire the **Animation** controller from **CtrlSpineNeck** to **BoneHead** to create double rotation on the head.

3. Wire the **Animation** controller from **CtrlSpineMid** to **BoneSpine04** to create double rotation on the upper spine.

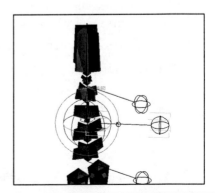

4. Test the two new portions of the rig by rotating each of the new control objects. The bone just above the control should rotate when you rotate the control object, and the bone above that one should rotate by double the amount. Undo any rotation before continuing.

## Finish the Spine Rig

Now you can link the whole spine rig together to make it work as a whole. Each of the new control objects must be linked to its next lower spine bone.

1. Link **CtrlSpineNeck** to **BoneSpine04**.

   Another strange occurrence: The head lies down on its side! The linkage has caused strange problems with the rig. To get around this problem, you can make the linkage part of the **Pose** controller for each control object. To do this, you will set the current controller to **Pose**, do the linking, then set the controller back to **Animation**.

2. Undo the last linking action.

3. Select **CtrlSpineNeck**.

4. On the **Motion** panel, double-click the **Pose** controller in the Rotation List rollout to make it the current controller.

5. Link **CtrlSpineNeck** to **BoneSpine04**.

   This time, the head stays put.

6. With **CtrlSpineNeck** selected, double-click the **Animation** controller in the Rotation List rollout to make it the current controller again.

7. Repeat this operation for **CtrlSpineMid**, linking it to **BoneSpine02** while the **Pose** controller is active. Set the active controller back to **Animation**.

   You now have a linked chain from the top of the head to the bottom of the spine that includes both bones and control objects.

8. Test the rig by rotating the control objects. You can rotate the entire spine by rotating the control object at the base of the spine, and you can increase the rotation for any joint along the way by rotating its control object.

   Undo any rotation you have done before continuing.

9. Save the scene as **CharRig13.max**.

## TOOLS REVIEW

Let's go do a brief review of the rigging tools you've learned so far.

*Bones* - The objects that make up the skeletal structure.

*Transform* - Move, rotate, or scale.

*Pivot Point* - XYZ axes that set the origin point and direction for transforms.

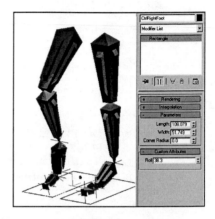

*Linking* - Connecting one object to another so one is the parent, and the other is the child.

*IK Chain* - A special control for bone structures that allows you to use inverse kinematics on the bone structure, where transforming the child object affects the parent object.

*Custom Attribute* - A custom-made parameter that you can add to any object.

*Wiring* - Connecting two parameters in the scene so one changes the other.

*Controller* - A method of specifying how a particular transform will occur. Different controllers make different parameters available to the animator.

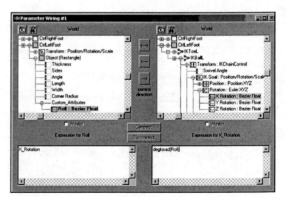

*List controller* - A special type of controller that lets you apply two or more controllers to one transform. The first controller holds the current transform information at the time the list controller is assigned, while later controllers can be used to animate the object.

At this point, you've learned enough rigging tools to complete the rest of the rig. I'll walk you through the process, but I won't give as much detail in the steps as I did before. Let's see if you can do it!

## Tutorial R9: Rigging the Wrist

The rig for the hands requires a little more work, but uses the same principles you've learned already.

You will rig the left wrist and hand first, then copy parts of the rig to the right side of the body later on. This will save you from having to rig both sides from beginning to end.

### Load the Scene

1. Load the file *CharRig13.max* that you created earlier, or load this file from the *Rigs* folder on the CD.

2. Unhide all the bones.

3. Hide the spine controls. You won't need them for a while, and they'll only get in the way.

### Create the Wrist Control

You will use an IK solver to rig the upper and lower arms.

1. Select **BoneUpperArmL**, the left upper arm bone. Choose *Animation menu > IK Solvers > HI Solver*, and click the palm bone to create an HI Solver for the left arm.

2. Name the new IK chain **IKWristL**.

If you like, you can move the IK chain around a little to ensure the palm is moving along with it. Undo any movements before continuing.

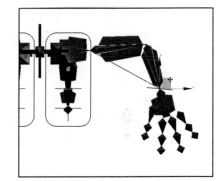

3. Choose *File menu > Merge*, and open the file *ControlShapes.max* on the *Rigs* folder on the CD. Merge the object **Gyro** from the file.

This is the shape made from three circles.

4. Name the gyro **CtrlWristL**.

5. Align the position of **CtrlWristL** with **IKWristL**.

Let's take a moment to consider what we're going to do with this control object. The most logical thing to do would be to link the IK chain to it, so you can bend the arm by moving the control object. But you also want to be able to rotate the hand by rotating the control object, so it would make sense to link the palm bone to the control object, too.

However, this would create a problem. The palm is part of the IK chain, so you can't link it to another object without breaking the chain. If you break the chain, **IKWristL** will no longer move the upper and lower arms.

To solve this problem, you'll use an *orientation constraint*. This is a type of controller that forces one object's rotation to always match another's.

To make the wrist rotation work intuitively with the orientation constraint, you'll need to align the control shape pivot point's orientation with the palm bone's pivot point. You can do this simply by aligning the orientation of the entire control shape.

### Assign the Orientation Constraint

1. Align the orientation of **CtrlWristL** to **BonePalmL**.

   This will rotate **CtrlWristL** so its pivot point has the same orientation as **BonePalmL**'s pivot point.

2. Select **BonePalmL**.

3. Choose *Animation menu > Constraints > Orientation Constraint*, and click **CtrlWristL**.

4. Test the constraint by rotating **CtrlWristL**. The palm should rotate in the same direction that the control shape rotates.

### Complete the Wrist Rig

1. Link the IK chain **IKWristL** to **CtrlWristL**.

2. Test the rig by moving **CtrlWristL**.

   The arm and hand should move together, and the elbow should bend. Undo any movements before continuing.

3. Save the scene as **CharRig14.max**.

### ☙ TIP ☙

*If aligning the orientation of one object with another aligns their pivot points' orientations, you might wonder why you didn't use this method to align the pivot points for the spine controls. The reason is that the spine controls point in a specific direction, and aligning their orientations with the bones might have caused them to point in different directions. With the gyro, you can rotate it by 90 degrees on any axis and it will still look the same.*

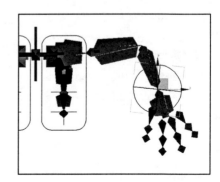

## FINGER ROTATIONS

Next, you will set up controls to make the fingers curl. Before you start this process, take a moment to work with your own hand. What are the most common poses you can make with your hand, and which fingers do you curl?

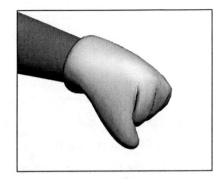

These are some the most commonly used poses:

- *Make a fist* - Curl all fingers into the palm, and curl the thumb across them

- *Point* - Curl all fingers into a fist except the index finger

- *Grasp an object* - Curl all fingers and thumb partway

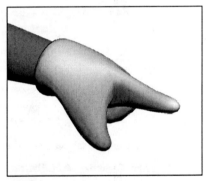

You usually pose your last three fingers the same way, either all curled or all uncurled. For example, it's pretty rare to curl your pinky without curling your second and third fingers. The exception would be curling all your fingers except the middle one to make a gesture that is unacceptable in polite company. Unless you plan to animate your character to make this gesture (and we won't be doing this in this book), you can safely set up the finger rig with just three curl controls: Thumb curl, index curl, and a curl for the remaining fingers.

When you curl your fingers, you will also see that the middle and end joints rotate more than the base joint. You will use expressions in the wiring to approximate this natural motion.

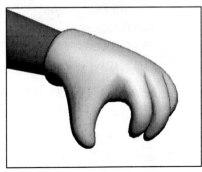

Here, you will rig the finger curls by creating custom attributes on the wrist control, then wiring them to the finger rotations.

## Determine the Curl Axis

Before wiring the parameters, let's look at the fingers' local axes to see which axis should be affected by the curl.

If one finger curls on a particular axis, all the finger bones will use the same axis for curling. This means you only have to test one finger bone to find out the correct axis of rotation for all the fingers.

1. Zoom in on the hand in the User or Perspective viewport.

2. Click **Select and Rotate**.

3. On the Main Toolbar, change the **Reference Coordinate System** to *Local*.

   The **Reference Coordinate System** drop-down menu is located just to the right of the **Select and Uniform Scale** button.

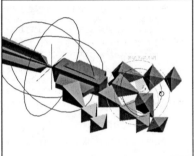

4. Rotate one of the fingers in the direction in which it should curl, and watch the number display above the transform gizmo to see which axis changes.

   The number display shows the degree of rotation as [X,Y,Z]. The numerical value will change for only one axis. In the rig included on the CD, the fingers curl on their local Y axes, but it's possible that yours are different.

5. Undo any rotation before continuing.

## Create Custom Attributes for Fingers

You will create three custom attributes on the wrist control to curl the fingers: One control for the index finger, and one for the two remaining fingers, and one for the thumb curl.

1. Select **CtrlWristL**.

2. Choose *Animation menu > Add Custom Attribute*.

3. For **Name**, enter **CurlTwoFingers**.

4. Enter a **Range** from **-20** to **200**.

5. Click **Add**.

> **☙ TIP ☙**
>
> *You might wonder how I came up with these ranges. It was simply through trial and error, trying different ranges until I found ones that worked well for the fingers.*
>
> *If you enter a range and find that it isn't right for the rig, you can't change it. You have two options: Delete the custom attribute and create it again, or use expressions in wiring to multiply or divide the attribute value and make it work with the rig.*
>
> *To delete a custom attribute, select the object, choose Animation menu > Add Custom Attribute, click the Delete button, and choose the attribute to delete.*

6. Create two more custom attributes with the following parameters:

**Name: CurlIndexFinger, Range: -20 to 200**
**Name: CurlThumb, Range: 0 to 120**

7. Close the Add Parameter dialog.

### Rig the Index Finger

To figure out the best wiring for the character's fingers, look at your own fingers again. The character has only one finger joint on each finger in addition to the knuckle joint, so we'll look at our own middle and knuckle joints and make the rig work as they do.

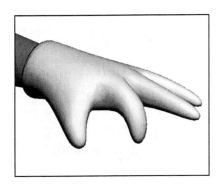

If you relax your hand then make a fist, you will see that the bone protruding from the knuckle doesn't really start rotating until the middle bone reaches an angle of about 70 degrees with the base joint. In addition, the middle joint never makes much more than a 90 degree angle with the base joint.

To approximate this motion, you will use expressions in the wiring to set up the following:

- *Middle bone* - Rotate to 90 degrees, then stop rotating

- *Base (knuckle) bone* - Start rotating only when middle bone rotation reaches 70 degrees

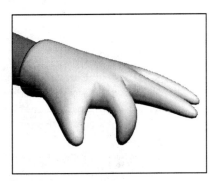

With this in mind, you're ready to rig the fingers. First, you'll wire the index finger's base bone rotation so it starts rotating only when **CurlIndexFinger** reaches a value of 70.

1. Hide all the finger nub objects. This will make it easier to see the finger curls after you rig them.

2. Select **CtrlWristL**, then right-click **CtrlWristL** and choose *Wire Parameters* from the Quad menu.

3. Wire the *CurlIndexFinger* custom attribute to the *Y Rotation* of **BoneIndex1L** with the following expression:

```
if (CurlIndexFinger < 70) then
   0;
else
   degtorad(CurlIndexFinger - 70);
```

> ### ☜ TIP ☞
> If your character's fingers curl on the X or Z axis, you should substitute the appropriate axis wherever Y Rotation is used for wiring.

Now you will wire the index finger's middle bone to rotate up to 90 degrees, then stop rotating.

4. Wire *CurlIndexFinger* to the *Y Rotation* of **BoneIndex2L** with the following expression:

```
if (CurlIndexFinger < 90) then
   degtorad(CurlIndexFinger);
else
   degtorad(90);
```

5. Test the wiring by increasing the **CurlIndexFinger** parameter to see how it affects the finger. The tip of the finger should reach the palm when **CurlIndexFinger** is at or near **200**.

### Wire the Remaining Finger Curls

1. Wire the **CurlTwoFingers** custom attribute to the middle and pinky fingers using expressions similar to those above. Use the chart below as a guide to which expression to use for which finger.

| Attribute | Bone | Axis | Expression |
|---|---|---|---|
| CurlTwoFingers | BonePinky1L | Y Rotation | if (CurlTwoFingers < 70) then... |
| CurlTwoFingers | BonePinky2L | Y Rotation | if (CurlTwoFingers < 90) then... |
| CurlTwoFingers | BoneMidfinger1L | Y Rotation | if (CurlTwoFingers < 70) then... |
| CurlTwoFingers | BoneMidfinger2L | Y Rotation | if (CurlTwoFingers < 90) then... |

2. Test the rig by increasing **CurlTwoFingers**. The fingers should curl into the palm when **CurlTwoFingers** reaches around **200**.

3. Save the scene as **CharRig15.max**.

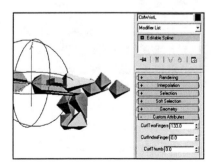

## THUMB ROTATION

Your thumb is one of the most evolved joints on your body. Only primates have opposable thumbs, which humans and monkeys can use to pick up and manipulate objects. Such everyday things as pencils, doorknobs, and buttons are designed for use with opposable thumbs.

Figuring out the thumb rotation for the rig requires more research into how a real hand works. Fortunately, you have all the research materials you need right in your hands.

There are two poses the character's thumb should be able to make:

*Grasp* - Curl the thumb partway to hold an object

*Fist* - Curl the thumb across the fingers

Let's research the *Grasp* pose. While looking at your own hand, pose your hand with your thumb and fingers straight out to make your hand nearly flat, then cup your thumb and fingers as if to grasp a cup or bottle. Do this gesture a few times, and observe your thumb closely. You will see that:

- You can rotate the base thumb joint (the one close to your wrist) along any axis, or swivel it in an arc.

- The second and third thumb bones rotate on only one axis.

- The last thumb bone can rotate by only about 60 degrees in relationship to its parent bone.

From the *Grasp* position, you can make a fist by curling your fingers into your palm and rotating your thumb slightly toward the fingers. If you use this pose for the character's fist, you will be able to wire the parameters in such a way that the thumb passes through the grasping position, then makes a fist. This might not exactly the way you make a fist in real life, but it will work just fine for our simple character, and will make the rig very versatile with a minimum of wiring.

In order to wire this type of rotation, you'll need to experiment with the thumb bones on the rig to see how they should rotate. Then you can write expressions for the thumb bones to make them form these poses when you animate the CurlThumb parameter.

To aid in this task, you'll animate both the thumb and finger bones to form the *Grasp* and *Fist* poses.

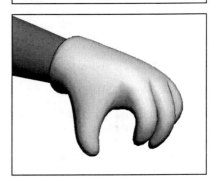

## Tutorial R11: Determining the Thumb Rotation

In this tutorial, you will animate the thumb bones manually to form the *Grasp* and *Fist* poses. Then you will look at the animated rotation angles to determine the expressions for rigging the thumb bone rotations to the **CurlThumb** parameter.

### Animate the Grasp Pose

1. Load the file *CharRig15.max* that you created earlier, or load this file from the *Rigs* folder on the CD.

2. Go to frame 10.

3. Turn on **Auto Key**.

4. Select **CtrlWristL**.

5. Increase **CurlTwoFingers** and **CurlIndexFinger** to about 110 to make the fingers form the grasping pose.

6. Rotate the thumb bones individually to complete the grasping pose.

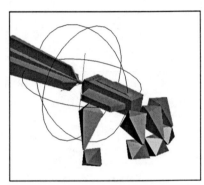

   The character has only two thumb bones, so you're limited in what you can do with them. Still, you should be able to get a reasonably accurate grasping pose from the two bones and the fingers.

   If you have difficulty with this step, load the file *ThumbPoses.max* from the *Rigs* folder on the CD, and look at the left hand's pose on frame 10.

### Animate the Fist Pose

1. Go to frame 20.

2. Select **CtrlWristL**.

3. With **Auto Key** turned on, increase **CurlTwoFingers** and **CurlIndexFinger** to about 170 to make the fingers curl into the palm.

4. Rotate the base thumb bone to make a fist.

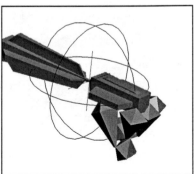

   Again, because the character has only two thumb bones, you're limited in what you can do. Make the pose look like a fist as much as you can without making the bones intersect one another.

   You can see an example of a fist pose in the file *ThumbPoses.max* from the *Rigs* folder on the CD. The fist pose is shown at frame 20.

## Determine the Thumb Rotation Values

Next, you will use the Trackbar at the bottom of the screen to help you determine the thumb rotation angles. The Trackbar shows the frame numbers, and any keys that have been set. You will see keys at frames 0, 10, and 20.

1. Select the base thumb bone.

2. Go to frame 10.

3. On the Trackbar, right-click the key at frame 10, and choose *BoneThumb1L: X Rotation* from the pop-up menu.

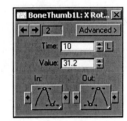

A dialog appears, showing you information about the bone at this frame. The **Value** parameter shows the current X rotation angle for the bone. You can change **Value** to change the amount by which the bone rotates around the X axis.

Most likely, **Value** is not set to a round number. To simplify the process of rigging the thumb, your goal is to find a series of round numbers for the X, Y, and Z rotation angles that will result in a reasonably realistic grasping motion.

4. Set **Value** to the nearest round number ending in 0 or 5. For example, if **Value** is **31.2**, change it to **30**. Note the number on a piece of paper, and close the dialog.

5. Right-click the key again, and choose *BoneThumb1L:Y Rotation*. Change **Value** to the nearest round number. Note the number and close the dialog.

6. Do the same for the Z rotation **Value**.

7. Select the second thumb joint. Right-click the key at frame 10, and go through the same process for this bone's **Value** numbers, changing each to the nearest round number and noting the number.

Does the grasping pose still look good? If not, you will have to change the numbers to get it to look right. You can change a rotation angle by changing the appropriate **Value** parameter right on the dialog. Unfortunately, you can't have more than one dialog active at a time, so you'll have to open each one individually as you need it.

---

☀ **TIP** ☀

---

*There are numerous ways to set up thumb rotation. This is the simplest method that will yield decent results for the two hand poses used in this book.*

8. Go to frame 20, and right-click the key at frame 20 to inspect the X, Y and Z rotation values for both the base and second thumb bones. Change the values to round numbers, and see if you can come up with a set of numbers that will work well with the first set of values.

You might need to go back and change some of the values on frame 10 to come up with a good set that will work.

For example, these are the numbers I came up with for my character (after a considerable amount of fiddling with the values on both frames 10 and 20):

| | BoneThumb1L | | | BoneThumb2L | | |
|---|---|---|---|---|---|---|
| Frame | 0 | 10 | 20 | 0 | 10 | 20 |
| X: | 0 | -20 | 20 | 0 | 0 | 0 |
| Y: | 0 | 60 | 60 | 0 | 0 | 0 |
| Z: | 0 | -30 | 30 | 0 | 60 | 60 |

**☙ TIP ☙**

To see the thumb curl I used to get these numbers, load the file *ThumbPoses.max* from the *Rigs* folder on the CD.

I looked for numbers that would look good on the thumb, and that would wire fairly easily. The **CurlThumb** custom attribute can range from 0 to 120, and 120 is divisible by each of these numbers. This will make the wiring process fairly straightforward.

9. When you have completed this process, save your scene as **ThumbPoses.max**.

## THUMB ROTATION EXPRESSIONS

To figure out the best way to wire thumb expressions, you'll need to make a chart similar to the one on the previous page. Here, I will come up with expressions for the chart I created. The first time you read through this section, follow along with my chart. Afterward, you can apply what you've learned to your own values to create your own expressions.

Let's take a closer look at the chart. I've added an extra line that shows the proposed values for CurlThumb for each pose.

|  |  | BoneThumb1L |  |  |  | BoneThumb2L |  |  |
|---|---|---|---|---|---|---|---|---|
| **Frame** |  | **0** | **10** | **20** |  | **0** | **10** | **20** |
|  | **X:** 0 | -20 | 20 | **X:** | 0 | 0 | 0 |
|  | **Y:** 0 | 60 | 60 | **Y:** | 0 | 0 | 0 |
|  | **Z:** 0 | -30 | 30 | **Z:** | 0 | 60 | 60 |
| **CurlThumb:** | 0 | 60 | 120 |  | 0 | 60 | 120 |

The custom attribute CurlThumb can range from 0 to 120. We want the thumb to form the *Grasp* pose when CurlThumb is 60, then go on to the *Fist* pose when CurlThumb is 120.

The values for BoneThumb2L: X Rotation and Y Rotation are always 0, so we don't need to wire them. Let's take them off the chart so we can focus on the values that do need to be wired.

|  |  | BoneThumb1L |  |  |  | BoneThumb2L |  |  |
|---|---|---|---|---|---|---|---|---|
| **Frame** |  | **0** | **10** | **20** |  | **0** | **10** | **20** |
|  | **X:** 0 | -20 | 20 |  |  |  |  |
|  | **Y:** 0 | 60 | 60 |  |  |  |  |
|  | **Z:** 0 | -30 | 30 | **Z:** | 0 | 60 | 60 |
| **CurlThumb:** | 0 | 60 | 120 |  | 0 | 60 | 120 |

Next, look at the chart and find the values that will be easiest to wire. For example, BoneThumb1L: Y rotation and BoneThumb2L: Z rotation both go to 60 when CurlThumb is 60, then remain at 60 no matter how high CurlThumb goes.

| | BoneThumb1L | | | BoneThumb2L | | |
|---|---|---|---|---|---|---|
| Frame | 0 | 10 | 20 | 0 | 10 | 20 |
| X: | 0 | -20 | 20 | | | |
| Y: | 0 | 60 | 60 | | | |
| Z: | 0 | -30 | 30 | Z: 0 | 60 | 60 |
| CurlThumb: | 0 | 60 | 120 | 0 | 60 | 120 |

These values will be easy to wire--just write an expression that uses the actual CurlThumb value up to 60, then leave the rotation at 60 for values beyond 60.

```
if (CurlThumb < 60) then
  degtorad(CurlThumb);
else
  degtorad(60);
```

Let's take those off the chart so we can see what we have left.

| | BoneThumb1L | | |
|---|---|---|---|
| Frame | 0 | 10 | 20 |
| X: | 0 | -20 | 20 |
| Z: | 0 | -30 | 30 |
| CurlThumb: | 0 | 60 | 120 |

You'll have to give the remaining expressions a little thought. These values have to go down from 0 to a negative number, then up to a positive number.

Here's where I got out my pad and pencil and worked on the numbers to see what would work. I tackled the Z rotation first since it has to go from 0 to -30 to 30, and these numbers go nicely into 60 and 120.

This is the expression I came up with for BoneThumb1L's Z rotation:

```
if (CurlThumb < 60) then
  - degtorad(CurlThumb / 2);
else
  degtorad(CurlThumb - 90);
```

How this expression works might not seem immediately obvious. Since you'll have to come up with your own expressions in the future, I'll tell you a little about how I came up with this particular one.

First, I made a list of several of the values CurlThumb could have, in order from 0 to 120. I listed the values 0, 30, 60, 90, and 120, with the idea that the progression of these values would give me a good idea of what needed to happen as CurlThumb increased.

Then I wrote down the desired Z rotation next to each CurlThumb value.

| CurlThumb | Z Rotation | |
|---|---|---|
| 0 | 0 | (Original pose) |
| 30 | -15 | |
| 60 | -30 | (*Grasp* pose) |
| 90 | 0 | |
| 120 | 30 | (*Fist* pose) |

Let's look at the CurlThumb values from 0 to 60. There's a pretty obvious expression you can use for this range:

```
if (CurlThumb < 60) then
  - degtorad(CurlThumb / 2);
```

This divides CurlThumb in half and makes it negative. So far, so good.

Next, take a look at the values from 60 to 120. Note that the Z rotation value for these values is always CurlThumb - 90. So you can write the second half of the expression as follows:

```
else
  degtorad(CurlThumb - 90);
```

The first half of the expression uses division, while the second half uses subtraction. If you paid attention in Algebra class, you know that strange things can happen when you mix one class of operators (multiplication and division) with another (addition and subtraction).

To make sure the expression will work, you want to take a close look at what happens when CurlThumb reaches 60 and has to switch from one type of operator to the other. The easiest way to do this is to calculate the Z rotation that both equations would produce when CurlThumb is 60. In this case, we find that both the first and second expressions return a Z rotation of -30. This is a good sign that the expression will work.

For the X rotation values, I made another list of corresponding values for CurlThumb and the X rotation:

| CurlThumb | X Rotation | |
|-----------|-----------|--------------------|
| 0 | 0 | (Original pose) |
| 30 | -10 | |
| 60 | -20 | (Grasp pose) |
| 90 | 0 | |
| 120 | 20 | (Fist pose) |

☙ **TIP** ☙

*Professional riggers use Algebra every day.*

For CurlThumb values under 60, I found I could use an expression similar to the one I used for the Z rotation:

```
if (CurlThumb < 60) then
  - degtorad(CurlThumb / 3);
```

For the values from 60 to 120, I saw that the values progress from -20 to 20, which is similar to the Z rotation progression of -30 to 30. Since 20 is 2/3 of 30, I realized I could use the same expression I used for the Z rotation, but simply multiply the subtraction result by 2/3:

```
else
  degtorad((CurlThumb - 90) * (2 / 3);
```

If you plug a CurlThumb value of 60 into both expressions, you will find that both result in -20, the correct X rotation value for the Grasp pose.

If you want to use rotation values other than the ones provided here, you'll need to work out expressions for these values. In the next tutorial, you'll use the values and expressions shown here.

## Tutorial R12: Wiring the Thumb Curl

With your carefully designed Algebraic expressions in hand, you can confidently go forth and wire the thumb bones' rotations to the **CurlThumb** parameter.

### Set up the List Controller

Before animating the thumb, you'll need to add a **Rotation List** controller to the thumb base. You'll be rotating this bone on all three axes, and it's already been posed on at least one axis, so the list controller will keep the animation values from interfering with the pose.

1. Load the file *CharRig15.max* that you created earlier, or load this file from the *Rigs* folder on the CD.

2. Select the base thumb bone, **BoneThumb1L**. On the **Motion** panel, assign a **Rotation List** controller as the **Rotation** controller, and set up two **Euler XYZ** controllers. Name them **Pose** and **Animation**, and make sure **Animation** is set as the active controller.

### Wire the Thumb Rotation

1. Select **CtrlWristL**.

2. Wire **CurlThumb** to **BoneThumb1L**'s *Y Rotation* (on the *Animation* controller), using the following expression:

```
if (CurlThumb < 60) then
   degtorad(CurlThumb);
else
   degtorad(60);
```

3. Wire **CurlThumb** to **BoneThumb2L**'s *Z Rotation* with the same expression you used in the previous step.

4. Wire **CurlThumb** to **BoneThumb1L**'s *Z Rotation* on the *Animation* controller, using the following expression:

```
if (CurlThumb < 60) then
   -degtorad(CurlThumb / 2);
else
   degtorad(CurlThumb - 90);
```

5. Wire *CurlThumb* to **BoneThumb1L**'s *X Rotation* on the *Animation* controller with the following expression:

```
if (CurlThumb < 60) then
   -degtorad(CurlThumb / 3);
else
   degtorad((CurlThumb - 90) * (2 / 3));
```

> ☙ **TIP** ☙
>
> *You don't have to put spaces between each operand when you enter the expression, but I find the expressions are easier to read and edit when entered this way.*

## Test the Wiring

It will be easier to test the wiring if you set the animation length to a lower number.

1. Click **Time Configuration**, and set **Length** to 100.

2. Select **CtrlWristL**.

3. Turn on **Auto Key**, and go to frame 10.

4. On the **Modify** panel, set **CurlTwoFingers** and **CurlIndexFinger** to 110, and increase **CurlThumb** to **60**.

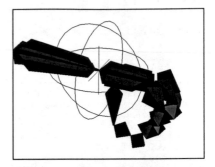

The thumb's pose should closely resemble the *Grasp* pose you animated earlier.

5. Go to frame 20, and set **CurlTwoFingers** and **CurlIndexFinger** to 170, and increase **CurlThumb** to 120.

Now the thumb's pose should resemble the *Fist* pose.

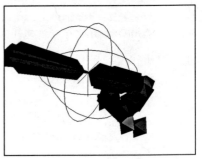

6. Turn off **Auto Key**.

7. Scrub the time slider back and forth, and watch the thumb as it animates.

8. Save the scene as **CharRig16.max**.

## Tweak a Simple Expression

There might be a slight twitch in the thumb as **CurlThumb** passes through 60. Right now, all the expressions change when **CurlThumb** reaches 60, which can make it look a little robotic, and also cause a twitch. You can alleviate this situation by altering the expressions slightly.

### ☙ TIP ☙

The term "tweak" means "to make slight adjustments". Both the rigging and animation processes often requires you to tweak values here and there.

The least complicated expression **BoneThumb1L**'s Y Rotation expression, so you'll tweak this one first.

1. Select the base thumb bone, **BoneThumb1L**.

2. Right-click the Trackbar, and choose *Controller Properties > BoneThumb1L:Y Rotation* from the pop-up menu.

The Parameter Wiring dialog appears with the wired parameters already displayed and highlighted. The rotation expression is displayed on the left when you access the dialog in this way.

3. Where the number **60** is used in the expression, replace it with **63**.

   This will cause the Y rotation to switch from the first expression to the second when **CurlThumb** reaches 63, which will offset it slightly from the other rotation axes.

4. Click **Update**.

5. Scrub the time slider and watch the animation around frame 10.

   The motion around frame 10 is a little less robotic, but still twitches slightly on the X rotation. You'll tweak that expression to ease the twitch.

## Tweak a Complex Expression

1. Right-click the Trackbar again, and choose *Controller Properties > BoneThumb1L > X Rotation* from the pop-up menu.

2. Replace the expression **(2/3)** with **(0.66)**.

   The value of 2/3, expressed in decimals, is 0.666666, with the 6's going on into infinity. By replacing 2/3 with 0.66, a slightly smaller number than 2/3, the rotation will change slightly.

3. Click **Update.**

4. Scrub the time slider and watch the thumb rotation around frame 10.

   If you've used the same numbers I did throughout this tutorial, the twitch should be gone.

   Feel free to experiment and play with the thumb rotation until you're satisfied with the results. Close the Parameter Wiring dialog when you're done.

5. Save the scene as **CharRig17.max**.

> ☙ **TIP** ☙
>
> If the Parameter Wiring dialog is still open, you can simply highlight X Rotation on the left side of the dialog.

> ☙ **TIP** ☙
>
> In CharRig17.max on the CD, I also changed the expression on BoneThumb2L's Z Rotation to use the number 57 instead of 60. This also served to make the rotation less robotic when CurlThumb reaches 60.

To complete the arm rig, you need a shoulder control and an elbow control. You will also need to copy the left arm rig to the right side.

### Rig the Shoulder

The control for the shoulder will work a little differently from the wrist control. It will be the parent object for the entire arm including the clavicle, but it will be positioned between the clavicle and the upper arm. In addition, its pivot point will be aligned with the clavicle's pivot point.

This might seem like a strange construction for the shoulder rig, but once it's set up, you'll see how this helps you control the shoulder.

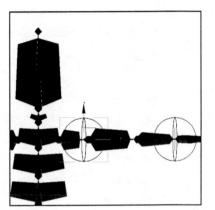

1. Continue from the previous tutorial, or load the file *CharRig17.max* that you created earlier. You can also load this file from the *Rigs* folder on the CD.

2. If necessary, go to frame 0 and turn off **Auto Key**.

3. Choose *File menu > Merge* to merge the **Gyro** object from *ControlShapes.max*.

   You could copy the wrist gyro to make the shoulder gyro, but then the shoulder gyro would have all the wrist's custom attributes on it. By merging it again, you start with a fresh gyro.

 4. Use **Align** to align the control object's position with the position of **BoneUpperArmL**, the left upper arm. Choose **Pivot Point** for the Current Object and Target Object.

   This aligns the control object's position with the upper arm.

5. Name the gyro **CtrlShoulderL**.

 6. On the **Hierarchy** panel, click **Affect Pivot Only**.

 7. Click **Align**, then click the left clavicle, **BoneClavicleL**. Align both the position and orientation. Choose **Pivot Point** for the Current Object and Target Object.

   This aligns the control object's pivot point with the clavicle's pivot point.

 8. Turn off **Affect Pivot Only**.

 9. Link **BoneClavicleL** to **CtrlShoulderL**.

### Test the Shoulder Rig

1. Turn on **Auto Key**.

2. Go to frame 10.

3. In the Front viewport, move the left wrist control, **CtrlWristL**, upward to extend the arm up, and rotate the wrist control to pose the hand comfortably.

   The shoulder looks stiff and unnatural.

4. In the Front viewport, rotate **CtrlShoulderL** to raise the shoulder.

   This pose looks more natural with the shoulder rotated upward.

   In essence, you are using the control object as a parent for the clavicle. You put the control object between the clavicle and upper arm simply to make it easier to select.

5. Turn off **Auto Key**.

### Rig the Elbow

The swivel angle for the wrist IK chain, **IKWristL**, controls the elbow's swivel. You will wire the swivel angle to a custom attribute on the wrist control so you can change it easily.

1. Go to frame 10.

2. Select **IKWristL**, and go to the **Motion** panel.

3. Test the **Swivel Angle** to figure out the best range for the custom attribute.

   For the rig included on the CD, the range of **-130** to **90** will work well.

4. Select **CtrlWristL**, and choose *Animation menu > Add Custom Attribute*.

5. On the Add Parameter dialog, enter **ElbowSwivel** as the name, and enter the range you determined when you tested the swivel angle. Click **Add** to add the parameter, and close the Add Parameter dialog.

6. Click **Time Configuration**, and set **Length** back to **10000**.

7. Wire the *ElbowSwivel* parameter to **IKWristL** > *Transform* > *Swivel Angle*, using the expression **degtorad(ElbowSwivel)**.

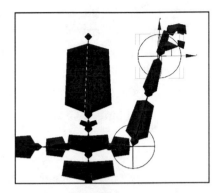

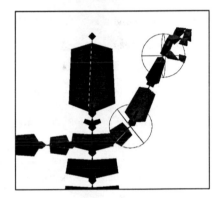

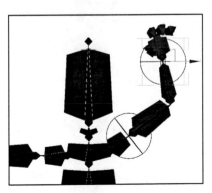

8. To test the elbow swivel rig, go to frame 10, turn on **Auto Key**, and change the **ElbowSwivel** parameter.

   Be sure to turn off **Auto Key** when you have finished testing the new custom attribute.

9. Save the scene as **CharRig18.max**.

**Pose the Finger Curls**

Before copying the rig to the right side of the body, you'll need to pose the finger curls. This will save you from having to do it again on the right side.

You will need to see the character mesh while you pose the finger curls, so you can fit the fingers inside the mesh.

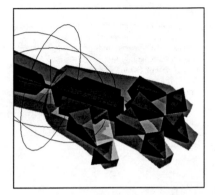

1. Unhide the character mesh, and freeze it.

2. Turn on **Auto Key** and go to frame 0.

3. Select **CtrlWristL**,

4. Adjust the curl attributes so the fingers curl to match the character mesh. If the fingers don't curl to sit inside the mesh, you can rotate the bones manually on the X or Z axes.

   If you can't get the finger bones posed correctly with the custom attributes, you can turn off **Auto Key** and modify the mesh at the **Vertex** sub-object level to fit the bones. Since you'll be able to curl or open the fingers at will after they're skinned, the initial pose is not so important.

   You also could have put a list controller on each bone before wiring it. Then the initial finger pose would have been the pose when all the custom attributes were 0. In this case, you would have put a range on the custom attribute from a negative to positive number, such as -30 to 90. When the custom attributes were at a negative value, the fingers would straighten out.

5. Turn off **Auto Key**.

6. Save the scene as **CharRig19.max**.

☙ **TIP** ☙

*Use Arc Rotate Selected to rotate around the User viewport and see the hand from all angles as you adjust the finger curls. This way, you can be sure the finger bones are going right through the mesh fingers. This feature rotates the view around the selected object, CtrlArmR. You can choose Arc Rotate Selected by clicking and holding the Arc Rotate button. The Arc Rotate Selected button includes a white circle. You will probably have to rotate the view and make adjustments several times before you're satisfied with the result.*

## Copy the Left Arm Rig

Now that you've set up custom attributes for the left arm, you can mirror the setup to the right side without having to rewire the entire right hand. If you mirror the left hand and its wrist control, the custom attributes will remain wired to the fingers, which will save you a lot of time.

1. Go to frame 0.

2. In the Front viewport, select all the left arm and hand bones, and the wrist and shoulder control objects. **Do not select the IK chain IKWristL.**

3. In the Top viewport, make a copy of the hand bones and wrist control below the original. To do this, hold down **[Shift]** while moving the selected objects.

Before you mirror the bones and control object to the right side, you will need to clean it up a little. The wrist and shoulder controls still contain the animation you created earlier.

4. Select the newly copied wrist control. On the trackbar, select and delete the keys on frames 10 and 20 for this object. To do this, draw a selection region around the keys, then right-click any key and choose *Delete Selected Keys* from the pop-up menu.

5. Using the same technique, delete the keys on frame 10 for the newly copied shoulder control.

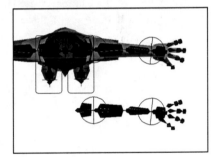

> ### ☙ TIP ☙
> *It is very important that you do NOT select the IK chain before copying and mirroring the hand. If you select this object, the copying and mirroring operations will not work as expected.*

## Mirror the Arm Rig

1. Delete all the right arm and hand bones.

2. Select the newly copied bones and control object.

3. Set the **Reference Coordinate System** to **World**.

4. Set the transform center to **Use Transform Coordinate Center**.

This will cause the arm to mirror across the grid. The character is standing at the center of the grid, so mirroring the arm will cause it to go to the other side of the body.

5. On the Main Toolbar, click **Mirror Selected Objects**. On the dialog, choose **X** as the Mirror Axis, and **No Clone** for Clone Selection. Click **OK**.

6. Change the transform center back to **Use Selection Center**.

7. Move the mirrored bones and the control object into place on the right side of the rig. Check your work in the Top viewport to make sure the arm is aligned properly.

8. In the Top viewport, zoom in on the hand. If you created your character symmetrically, the finger bones should line up with the character's fingers. If they don't, rotate the finger bones on the local Z axis to make them fit.

### Rename the Right Arm Objects

When you mirrored and copied the arm bones and controls, they were each given the same object name with **L01** on the end instead of just **L**. Now you must rename them.

1. Change the names of the right hand bones to the same as those for the left, but with a **R** on the end instead of an **L**.

Press **[H]** to display a list of the objects in the scene, and type ***L01** in the entry area at the top of the Select Objects dialog. Click **Select** to select them. Then choose *Tools menu > Rename Objects*. On the Rename Object dialog, choose **Selected**. Turn on **Suffix** and **Remove Last**, and turn off all other options. Enter **R** for **Suffix**, and set the **Remove Last** number to **3**. Click **Rename** once, and close the dialog.

2. Press the **[H]** key to check the new object names, and make sure the new hand objects have the suffix **R**. Close the Select Objects dialog.

Now you will need to add these new arm bones to the **Bones** selection set.

3. Select the new arm bones. Do not select the control objects.

4. Choose *Edit menu > Named Selection Sets*. In the Named Selection Sets dialog, highlight **Bones**, and click **Add Selected Objects**. Close the dialog.

5. Save the scene as **CharRig20.max**.

### Recreate the Right Arm Rig

1. Recreate the HI Solver for the arm. Select the right upper arm bone, then choose *Animation menu > IK Solvers > HI Solver* and click the palm bone.

2. Name the new IK chain **IKWristR**.

3. Link **IKWristR** to **CtrlWristR**.

### Complete the Right Arm Setup

Let's take a look at the wrist's custom attributes and see how they responded to the mirroring process.

1. Select **CtrlWristR** and go to the **Modify** panel.

   All the custom attributes are there, and they all work on the mirrored fingers! However, you lost the **ElbowSwivel** wiring because you didn't mirror the IK solver for the arm.

2. Wire **CtrlWristR**'s *ElbowSwivel* parameter to **IKWristR** > *Transform* > *Swivel Angle*. Be sure to use the expression **degtorad(ElbowSwivel)**.

3. Link both **CtrlShoulderR** and **CtrlShoulderL** to **BoneSpine04**, the top spine bone.

### Test the Right Arm Rig

1. Click **Time Configuration**, and set **Length** back to **100**.

2. Unfreeze the character mesh, and hide it.

3. Go to frame 10, and turn on **Auto Key**.

4. Move and rotate **CtrlWristR** and **CtrlShoulderR** to raise the character's arm and match the left arm pose. You can also animate **ElbowSwivel** and the finger curls if you like.

In doing this, you might notice that the upper arm bone flips when you move the hand behind the character's head. Earlier, you kept the foot bone from flipping by setting its IK chain's **Parent Space** to **IK Goal**. But in this case, the IK goal is linked to the wrist control, which can rotate on any axis. Changing the **Parent Space** to **IK Goal** would make the IK goal rotate with the wrist control, which would cause strange problems in the rig.

To solve this problem, you will replace the link between the IK goal and the wrist control with a *position constraint*. This will cause the IK goal to follow the wrist control, but not rotate with it. Then you can set the **Parent Space** for the IK goal to **IK Goal**, and the upper arm bone will not flip.

5. Select **IKWristL**, and click **Select and Unlink**. Choose *Animation menu* > *Constraints* > *Position Constraint*, and click **CtrlWristL**.

6. In the **Motion** panel, set **Parent Space** to **IK Goal**.

7. Repeat the last two steps with the **IKWristR**.

8. On frame 10, correct the animation by adjusting each wrist's **ElbowSwivel** parameter, if necessary.

9. Save the scene as **CharRig21.max**.

To complete the rig, you just need an overall control for the legs, and a method for controlling the knee swivel.

### Create the Control for the Legs

1. In the Top viewport, create a circle shape about twice as wide as the character's body. Name the shape **CtrlLegs**.

2. Align the shape with **BoneSpine01**. In the Align dialog, set both Current Object and Target Object to **Pivot Point**.

3. Link the thigh bones to **CtrlLegs**.

4. Unhide the spine control objects.

5. Link the lowest spine control shape, **CtrlSpineBase**, to **CtrlLegs**.

### Test the Leg Rig

1. Go to frame 0, and remove the animation keys from **CtrlFootL** and **CtrlFootR**.

2. Go to frame 10, turn on **Auto Key**, and move **CtrlLegs** downward in the Front viewport.

   The character's knees will bend as you move **CtrlLegs** up and down, but the hands will not go with it. You can also rotate **CtrlLegs** to rotate both the thighs and the upper body.

   It is possible that one or both legs will bend the wrong way. If this happens, you can fix the problem by adjusting the swivel angle for the heel IK chain.

3. Turn off **Auto Key**.

4. On frame 10, select the IK goal at the heel for the leg that bends backwards.

5. On the **Motion** panel, set the **Swivel Angle** to 90, 180 or -90 to make the knee bend correctly.

### Wire the Knee Swivel

Now you will set up a custom attribute on each foot control to swivel the knee.

1. Select **CtrlFootL**.

2. Add a custom attribute named **KneeSwivel**, and give it a range from **-90** to **90**.

>
>
> **☃ TIP ☃**
>
> *Some riggers prefer to create a separate control to which the spine and leg controls are linked. This type of rig gives you the ability to rotate the thighs independent of the spine.*

3. Select **CtrlFootR**, and create the same custom attribute for this foot control.

4. Wire each of the **KneeSwivel** parameters to the **Swivel Angle** parameter on the corresponding heel's IK chain.

   If you had to change the **Swivel Angle** earlier to make the knee bend correctly, you will have to enter an expression that accommodates this. For example, if you had to set the **Swivel Angle** to 180, then you will have to use the expression **degtorad(KneeSwivel + 180)** to make the custom attribute work properly.

5. Test the rig by turning on **Auto Key** and changing the **KneeSwivel** parameter on frame 10.

6. Turn off **Auto Key** when you have finished testing the rig.

### Finish up the Rig

You need just one more item: A single object that controls the entire body, so you can easily move the entire character at once. This is essential for placing the character at the start of the animation.

1. In the Top viewport, create a large rectangle. Name it **CtrlBody**.

2. Position the rectangle at the bottom of the character's feet.

   Now, the only remaining task is to link up the wrist and shoulder controls.

3. Link **CtrlLegs**, **CtrlFootL** and **CtrlFootR** to **CtrlBody**.

4. Link **CtrlWristL** and **CtrlWristR** to **CtrlBody**.

5. Test the linkage by moving **CtrlBody**. When you move **CtrlBody**, the entire hierarchy should go with it. Undo any movements before continuing.

6. Select all the control objects (all objects beginning with **Ctrl**), and create a named selection set called **Control Objects**.

7. Save the scene as **CharRig22.max**.

   There are more controls you could add to this rig, but these will be sufficient for many types of animation. You will animate with this rig in the *Character Animation* chapter. But before you can do that, you'll need to skin the character with the tools and techniques described in the *Skinning* chapter.

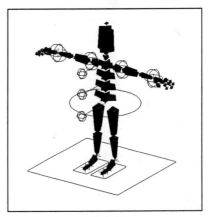

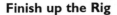

---

### ☙ TIP ☙

*If you prefer, you can link the wrist controls to CtrlLegs so the hands will move with the spine.*

# 3
# SKINNING

The process of associating
the bones with the mesh
is called *skinning*.

Technically speaking, skinning is part of the rigging process. However, it requires a set of tools and techniques quite different from those for setting up controls for bones.

## THE SKIN MODIFIER

In 3ds max, you start the skinning process by applying the Skin modifier to the mesh, and associating bones with the mesh. Each bone influences (deforms) the mesh around it when the bones are animated.

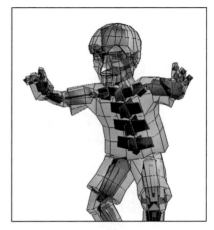

To perform the deformation, each vertex in the mesh receives a specific *weight* from each bone. If the bone completely controls the vertex, the vertex's weight with regard to that bone is 1.0. If the bone has no influence over the vertex, the vertex's weight for that bone is 0.0.

A weight between 0.0 and 1.0 means the vertex is affected by the bone to some degree. This partial weighting is used at joints such as the elbows, wrists, knees, and ankles. At the knee, for example, the vertices are affected by both the thigh and calf bones. A vertex at the top of the knee might have a weight of 0.7 for the thigh bone, and 0.3 for the calf. Usually, a vertex's weights for all its bones add up to 1.0.

There are two ways to set vertex weights: With envelopes, and with manual adjustment.

## ENVELOPES

By default, the Skin modifier creates two capsule-shaped areas around each bone called *envelopes*. The vertices that fall within a bone's envelopes are assigned a weight with regard to that bone. You can change the size and placement of envelopes to change the weights of vertices that fall inside it, but you cannot change an envelope's general shape.

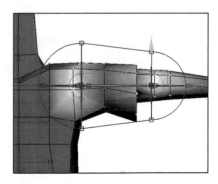

Envelopes are useful for roughing out the vertex weights. But with most character rigs, envelopes won't give you enough control over the weights to set up an accurate deformation, particularly at the joints.

## MANUAL VERTEX ADJUSTMENT

With any character that has arms and legs, you will need to adjust vertex weights manually. This is not as scary is it might seem. With a low-polygon mesh such as the one we use in this book, you'll be able to see the results of your manually-set weights instantly, and can work intuitively with the weights onscreen.

Manually-set vertex weights override any weights assigned by envelopes.

## ANGLE DEFORMERS

Another method for specifying how vertices deform is the *angle deformer*. This tool lets you manually move vertices to "show" them how to respond when the angle between two bones approaches or reaches a certain angle. For example, when the character's elbow bends by more than 90 degrees, you can use an angle deformer to "show" the Skin modifier how to keep the vertices at the inside of the elbow from pinching.

You will learn how to use all these tools in the practice exercise that follows.

### Practice P: USING THE SKIN MODIFIER

Here, you will practice using the **Skin** modifier on a simple object.

**Load the Scene**

1. Load the scene *Practice_Skin01.max* from the *Practice* folder on the CD.

   This scene contains a see-through cylinder with three bones. The bones are animated, but the **Skin** modifier has not been applied to the cylinder.

2. Pull the time slider to see the animation.

   The bones rotate until frame 25.

**Apply the Skin Modifier**

1. Go to frame 0.

   The frame on which you apply the **Skin** modifier is important. The **Skin** modifier uses the relationship between the bones and mesh on the current frame to determine the bones' initial influences over vertices.

2. Select the cylinder.

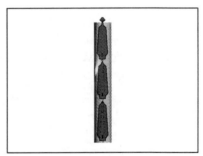

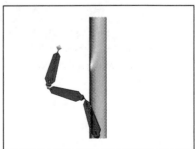

3. Go to the **Modify** panel, and apply the **Skin** modifier to the cylinder.

4. On the Parameters rollout, click **Add**. On the Select Bones dialog, select all the bones, and click **Select**.

Now the bones will influence the cylinder.

5. Pull the time slider to see how the mesh responds to the skinning.

The mesh bends with the bones. However, the mesh looks slightly crumpled at the joints, especially in the topmost joint, where the bending angle is about 90 degrees. This is typical of the situation you will encounter when you skin a character.

### Look at the Envelopes

1. Select the cylinder.

2. Press **[Alt-X]** to make the cylinder appear solid.

3. On the **Modify** panel, click **Edit Envelopes**.

The mesh turns blue, except for one area, which is red. Two capsule-shaped envelopes surround the red area.

4. In the Parameters rollout, select different bones to see their envelopes.

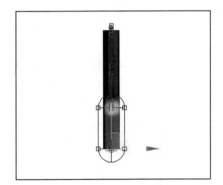

The initial sizes of the envelopes are determined by the sizes of the bones. If the bones are 1/2 to 3/4 the size of the mesh, the envelopes should encompass the mesh around it.

Of the pair of envelopes, one is completely inside the other. The one inside is called the *inner envelope*, while the other is the *outer envelope*.

Ideally, the inner envelope encompasses a non-bending part of the mesh, a place where a rigid bone would be. Outer envelopes are designed to overlap in joint areas, which causes the vertices in those areas to be influenced by both bones to some degree.

## Adjust the Envelopes

Each envelope has numerous square-shaped *handles* that define its shape. You can move the handles to change the size and shape of the envelope.

When you're shaping envelopes, the vertices and faces within the envelope change color to tell you whether they're being influenced by the bone, and by how much. Red vertices are completely influenced by the bone, with a weight of 1.0. Vertices and faces gradually change from red to orange to yellow as they are less influenced. Vertices and faces that receive no influence from the envelope, with a weight of 0.0, are blue.

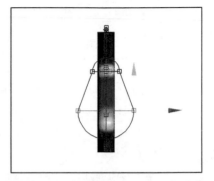

Even though the inner envelopes in this example do not encompass the mesh, the area around them is red. This is because no other bone is influencing that area, so the surrounding outer envelope gives these vertices a weight of 1.0.

1. On any envelope, drag one of the rectangular handles to change the size of an envelope.

   The mesh changes color accordingly, but the shape of the mesh doesn't change.

2. Pull the time slider to frame 25.

3. Select one of the envelopes that influences a joint.

4. Drag one of the handles near the joint to see how the change in the envelope affects the mesh.

   With joints, it's easier to see the effects of envelopes when the joint is bent. This is a very effective way to work. You can change envelopes on any frame to affect the skinning throughout the animation.

### ☀ TIP ☀

*When changing envelope sizes, make sure Auto Key is turned off. Envelope sizes can be animated, but in general, this is not desirable.*

### Adjust Envelope Directions

The envelope's handles lie on its *cross sections*. These are the circular shapes that set the volume of the envelope at that point. Each envelope also has *directional handles*, two gray handles at the each end of the inner envelope. You can move these handles to change the length of the envelope, or the direction in which the envelope lies.

It can be difficult to select directional handles unless you first turn off the ability to select cross section handles.

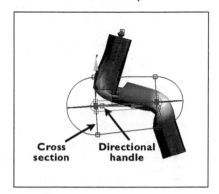

1. In the Parameters rollout, uncheck the **Cross Sections** option.

2. Select one of the gray handles at the end of an envelope. These are the only handles you are allowed to select.

3. Move the handle to change the direction in which the envelope lies.

   Most likely, this change will not improve the way the joints look. This step is given only to show you how to do this task, as you will need it when you skin the character.

   **Cross section    Directional handle**

4. Undo the change to the envelope direction.

5. Check **Cross Sections** to allow selection of the cross section handles.

6. Adjust the envelopes at frame 25 until the bends at the joints look as good as you can get them with this method.

   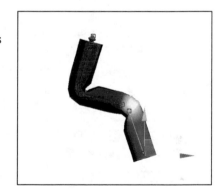

   Don't be concerned if the joints look crumpled or messy. You will fix this in the next set of steps.

7. Save the scene as **Practice_Skin02.max**.

### Select Vertices for Manual Adjustment

Now you will manually adjust the vertex weights to make the cylinder's joints look better when they bend. First, you will change the display to make it easier to see and select the appropriate vertices.

1. In the Parameters rollout, check **Vertices**.

   This will allow you to select vertices for manual adjustment.

2. Right-click the Front viewport label, and choose *Edged Faces* from the dropdown menu.

   This allows you to see the cylinder's vertices more clearly.

3. In the Parameters rollout, uncheck **Envelopes**.

   This will prevent you from accidentally selecting envelopes when you are working with the vertices.

4. In the Display rollout, check **Show No Envelopes**.

   This unclutters the screen so you can work more effectively. You can no longer select a bone by clicking it in a viewport, but you can still select a bone by highlighting its name in the Parameters rollout.

5. In the Parameters rollout, highlight **Bone01**.

   The first part of vertex weighting is to figure out which vertices need adjustment, then select them. This can be tricky. It is easiest to see which vertices need adjustment when the mesh is deformed. However, it is easiest to select the vertices when the mesh is not deformed.

   To select the appropriate vertices, you will look at the deformed mesh to locate them, then go back to frame 0 to select them. You will work with one row of vertices at a time.

6. Pull the time slider to frame 25, and watch the lowest joint closely in the Front viewport. Locate the vertices at the bend that will need adjustment.

7. Keeping your eye on the vertices, move the time slider back to frame 0.

8. Draw a selection region around the highest rows of vertices that require adjustment. These vertices are most likely yellow or orange.

   A white box appears around each selected vertex.

**Adjust Vertex Weights**

1. Go to frame 25.

2. On the **Modify** panel, locate the **Abs. Effect** parameter in the Weight Properties group.

   This is the parameter that sets the selected vertices' weight for the currently selected bone. The parameter name is short for *absolute effect*, which means it sets the vertex weights to exactly the value you enter. If the selected row of vertices have different weights (as they usually do when weights are set by envelopes), the parameter will not show a value at the moment.

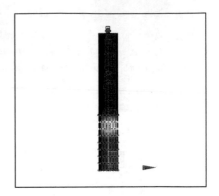

☼ **TIP** ☼

One way to keep track of the vertices that need to be adjusted is to note their colors. Vertices at joints are usually yellow, orange, or pink.

3. While watching the Front viewport, use the **Abs. Effect** spinner to increase or decrease this value until the vertices are angled slightly more than the vertices just above them. A value of **0.15** to **0.25** should work well.

4. Go back to frame 0, and select the next lowest row of vertices.

5. Go to frame 25, and change the **Abs. Effect** spinner so the vertices are angled slightly more than the first set.

    When you do this, you are actually setting two sets of weights. The weights for the selected bone are set to the value you set with **Abs. Effect**. The weights for the adjacent bone are adjusted accordingly, so the two sets of weights add up to 1.0.

    For example, if you set **Abs. Effect** to **0.35**, the vertices' weights for the adjacent bone will be automatically adjusted to **0.65**.

6. Repeat these steps on one or two more rows of vertices, until the joint looks smooth.

    Now you will adjust the other joint, which has a more severe bend.

7. In the Parameters rollout, highlight **Bone02**.

8. Use the same method you used before to determine which vertices need to be corrected. Select each row of vertices, and adjust the **Abs. Effect** parameter for each one until the joint looks as smooth as possible.

    With this joint, it's impossible to create a perfectly smooth bend. The angle is so severe that the joint is pinched. This looks unnatural, as the joint loses its original volume at this point.

    To correct this problem, you will use another skinning tool, the *joint angle deformer*.

9. Save the scene as **Practice_Skin03.max**.

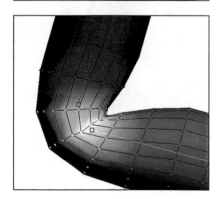

## Apply a Joint Angle Deformer

An *angle deformer* is a tool that applies custom deformation to vertices when adjacent bones approach or reach a certain angle. For example, with the topmost joint in the cylinder, the two bones are at an angle of about 90 degrees to one another. You can use an angle deformer to specify that the vertices at the joint should react in a certain way when the angle between the bones approaches or reaches 90 degrees.

Once an angle deformer is set up on a pair of bones, it will affect the vertices in the specified way throughout the animation. In other words, whenever the pair of bones are animated to approach or reach a 90 degree angle, the vertices will respond as specified by the angle deformer.

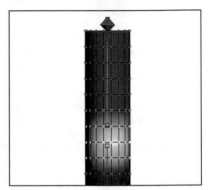

Here, you will use a *joint angle deformer*. This type of deformer is designed for use on joints such as elbows and knees, and is the easiest type to use.

1. Scrub back and forth between frames 0 and 25, and locate the vertices involved in the severe bend.

2. Select these vertices.

3. Select two additional rows of vertices, one above and one below the set of affected vertices.

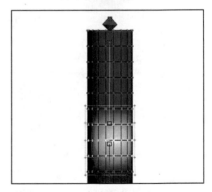

   When using an angle deformer, you won't get a chance to change the vertex selection after the deformer is applied. For this reason, it's always a good idea to select a larger area of vertices than you think you'll need.

   Although a joint angle deformer affects the vertices where two bones meet, you apply this type of angle deformer to the child bone of the pair.

4. In the Parameters rollout, highlight **Bone03**.

5. In the Gizmos rollout, make sure *Joint Angle Deformer* is selected from the dropdown list.

6. Click **Add Gizmo**.

   A yellow lattice (wireframe) appears around the selected vertices. If you go to frame 25, you will see that the vertices are pushed into a stiff formation at this frame.

## ☼ TIP ☼

*It doesn't matter what frame you're on when you add the gizmo.*

In the Gizmo Parameters rollout, the names of the two affected bones are displayed, along with the current angle between the two bones. Note that an angle of 180 means the bones go in a straight line relative to one another, as they do at frame 0. The angle between the bones changes from 180 to about 90 degrees by frame 25.

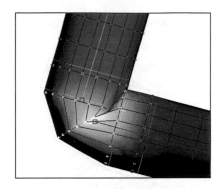

You will edit the lattice to show the angle deformer how you want the vertices to respond when the bones approach and reach this angle.

### Edit the Lattice

1. In the Parameters rollout, uncheck **Vertices**.

    This will prevent you from accidentally selecting vertices instead of lattice points.

2. Right-click the Front viewport label, and choose *Wireframe*.

    This will make it easier to see the lattice points.

3. In the Display rollout, uncheck **Show Colored Vertices**.

    This will also make it easier to see and select the lattice points.

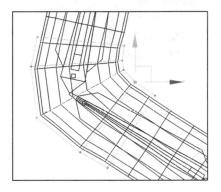

4. In the Gizmo Parameters rollout, click **Edit Lattice**.

5. In the Front viewport, scrub the time slider and look for the first frame where the elbow starts to pinch severely. This will most likely be around frame 15.

6. Select and move the points on the lattice to smooth out the elbow joint.

    This sets a key for the lattice at this angle. When the lattice reaches an angle for which a key is set, the vertices appear in red.

7. Continue scrubbing to later and later frames, and move the lattice points to smooth out the elbow joint.

8. Finish off the adjustment by smoothing out the joint at frame 25.

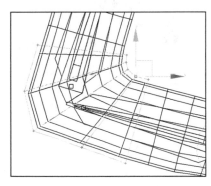

    If the lattice lines overlap at this frame, you will have to "untangle" the lattice by moving the points away from one another.

    If you like, you can make the outer part of the bend bulge outward around frame 25 to create the look of an elbow bone.

### Adjust Intermediate Points

1. Scrub the time slider to see how the joint responds to the animation.

   At an intermediate frame, such as 5 or 10, you might find that the cylinder bulges out unnaturally.

2. Go to any frame between 10 and 15, and adjust the lattice points so the cylinder looks right for the degree of bend.

### Adjust the Joint Graph

> **☀ TIP ☀**
>
> *When selecting lattice points, draw a selection region around each point to select both the visible point and the one behind it.*

If the lattice "pops" or jiggles when you scrub the time slider, you can correct this problem by adjusting the keys you set for the joint angle deformer. You can see and edit the angle keys on the Joint Graph.

1. Click **Edit Angle Keys** Curves on the Gizmo Parameters rollout. The Joint Graph appears.

2. Scrub the animation while watching the Joint Graph, and watch the gray vertical line on the graph move.

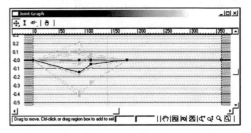

   Keys for the joint angle deformer are set according to the angle between the two bones, not the frame they were set on. The numbers across the top of the graph go from 0 to 360 to represent the bone's angle with its parent. The gray key lines show key settings that were current at one time or another while you adjusted the lattice.

   If any of the keys are too close together, this might cause the lattice to pop or jiggle. You can solve this problem by selecting and moving keys to a nearby angle to consolidate the two sets of keys, or by deleting a set of keys altogether.

3. Scrub the time slider back and forth, and make any necessary adjustments to the lattice or joint graph to make the animation look smooth.

4. In the Gizmo Parameters rollout, turn off **Edit Lattice**.

5. Turn off **Edit Envelopes**.

6. Save the scene as **Practice_Skin04.max**.

   If you like, you can test the angle deformer by animating **Bone03**. When this bone approaches or reaches a 90-degree angle with **Bone02**, the mesh will deform according to the lattice shape that you set with the angle deformer.

---

## CHARACTER SKINNING

So far, you have learned how to apply the Skin modifier, adjust vertex weights, and apply an angle deformer. When applying the Skin modifier to a character mesh, there are a few additional considerations.

### CHOOSING BODY PARTS FOR SKINNING

If two or more mesh parts are going to use the same skeletal structure, you can apply the Skin modifier to all the parts at once. For example, if your character's upper and lower body are separate objects, you can select both objects and apply the Skin modifier to both at the same time. This would create an *instanced modifier* on the modifier stack, where changing Skin parameters for one object would change them for all objects to which Skin was applied.

For the character in this book, you will apply the Skin modifier to the body only. You could apply it to the head and hair too, but this isn't necessary since the head and hair won't need to deform with the bones; most likely, you'll want the head to nod, shake, and tilt, but not deform.

Instead, you'll link the head mesh to the head bone, and animate the head by rotating the neck control.

> **TIP**
>
> *When working on your own characters, you might encounter situations where it's appropriate to apply the Skin modifier to the head. For example, you would do this if you wanted to animate the head bending or deforming.*

### MESHSMOOTH AND SKINNING

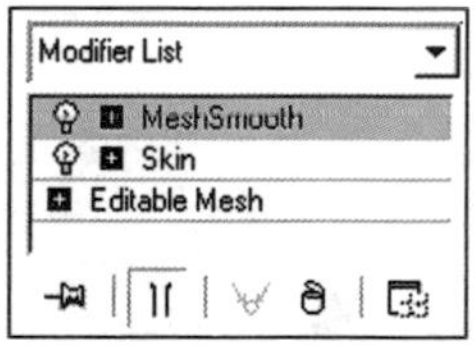


You will most likely want to apply the MeshSmooth modifier to a low-polygon character to smooth it out before rendering. However, you should put the Skin modifier *below* MeshSmooth on the stack. This minimizes the number of vertices you will have to adjust with the Skin modifier. You can apply the Skin modifier below MeshSmooth by highlighting the Editable Poly listing, then applying the Skin modifier.

When the modifiers are arranged in this way, the model still deforms correctly, and the result is beautifully smoothed. If you put the Skin modifier *above* MeshSmooth, you will only make more work for yourself, and the result will not be any better than if you put the Skin modifier below MeshSmooth.

In this book, you will apply the Skin modifier to a model that has no MeshSmooth modifier on it. After the skinning process is complete, you will apply the MeshSmooth modifier to the mesh and see the result.

## SKIN POSE

The Skin modifier relies on the placement of the bones in relationship to the mesh to make its associations correctly. Right now, the bones are placed correctly, but soon you'll be animating the rig.

Setting the *skin pose* allows you to return to the pose used for skinning at any time during the animation process. The skin pose saves the positions of bones, IK chains, and any control objects.

You can set the skin pose by choosing *Character menu > Set Skin Pose*. Later, if you need to make the bones return to the skin pose, you can choose *Character menu > Assume Skin Pose*.

Before we start skinning the character, let's set a skin pose for it.

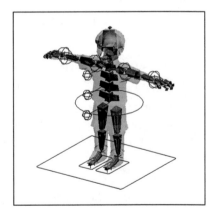

## Tutorial S1: SETTING THE SKIN POSE

### Check the Rig

1. Load the file *CharRig22.max* from your *Rigs* folder, or load it from *Rigs* folder on the CD.

2. If necessary, unhide and unfreeze all parts of the mesh.

3. If the character mesh isn't see-through, select all mesh parts and press **[Alt-X]** to make it so.

4. Check the model carefully to make sure the bones go through the appropriate parts of the mesh. The bones for the fingers and feet are the most likely ones to be out of place.

5. If necessary, put the bones in their correct locations by using the rig controls, or by moving or rotating the bones themselves.

### Set the Skin Pose

1. Select all the objects in the scene, including the bones, IK chains, control objects, and character mesh.

2. Choose *Character menu > Set Skin Pose*. When you are asked if you really want to set the skin pose, answer **Yes**.

3. Save the scene as **CharRig23.max**.

---

☀ **TIP** ☀

*To make the bones line up properly with the mesh, you can also alter the mesh itself.*

---

Now you're ready to apply the **Skin** modifier to the character and adjust its skinning. But first, a little preparation is in order.

### Prepare the Mesh for Skinning

1. Link the hair mesh to the head mesh.

2. Link the head mesh to **BoneHead**.

3. Select the character's body mesh. The head and hair should not be selected.

## ☼ TIP ☼

*By linking the hair and head meshes to the head bone, they will move with the rig when you test the Skin modifier in the next set of steps.*

If the **MeshSmooth** modifier has been applied to the body mesh, you will need to remove it before applying the **Skin** modifier, or apply the **Skin** modifier below **MeshSmooth**. Here, we'll remove it and put it back later.

4. If you have applied the **MeshSmooth** modifier to the body mesh, remove it by highlighting it in the modifier stack and clicking **Remove modifier from the stack**.

### Apply the Skin Modifier

1. Apply the **Skin** modifier to the mesh.

2. In the Parameters rollout, click **Add**. Select all the bones. You can do this easily by typing in the prefix **Bone** at the top of the dialog. Do not select IK chains, control objects, or any other objects in the scene.

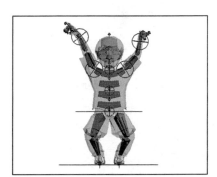

As you were rigging the character, you animated some parts of the rig to test the controls. Now you will use this animation to see how well the skinning is working.

3. Pull the time slider to see the current deformation.

If the mesh moves along with the bones in a general way, then you have associated the bones and mesh correctly.

You don't need the bones and control objects to be visible while you're adjusting envelopes, and they'll only get in the way, so you can hide them for now. You also don't need the head and hair to be visible.

4. Hide everything in the scene except the body mesh.

5. Turn off see-through mode for the mesh by pressing **[Alt-X]**.

## ☼ TIP ☼

*You might find it helpful to work in Smooth+Highlights mode, with Edged Faces turned on so you can see the vertex colors.*

## Look at the Envelopes

1. Go to frame 0.

2. Select the body mesh. In the Parameters rollout, click **Edit Envelopes**.

3. Click on various envelopes on the character to see what they look like.

   When you assigned the bones to the **Skin** modifier, you also included the nub bones. These bones are unnecessary for skinning, and could cause problems if their envelopes extend into the mesh.

4. In the Parameters rollout, highlight each bone that ends in **Nub**, and click the **Remove** button at the top of the rollout after highlighting each one.

   This removes the nubs from the skinning process, and saves you extra work.

## Perform Rough Adjustments on Envelopes

Now you can start adjusting the envelopes for the mesh.

Don't spend a lot of time puzzling over the envelopes at this point. The idea here is to quickly adjust them so they're roughly the right size for the mesh. You should spend no more than two or three minutes on each envelope.

1. Start your adjustments with the legs. Click the left thigh envelope, and adjust it so it encompasses the left thigh but not the right.

2. When you think you've done a decent job of it, click the **Copy** button in the Envelope Properties group.

3. Select the right thigh envelope, and click **Paste**. This pastes the copied envelope to the right thigh.

4. Next, click the left calf. Work with this envelope for a few minutes, then copy and paste it to the other side.

5. Continue on with the feet, arms, head, and spine, copying and pasting envelopes when you can.

6. In the Top viewport, zoom in on the fingers, and adjust their envelopes.

   If an envelope looks okay to you, or if you're not sure, leave it and go on to the next one. You're looking only for envelopes that obviously need adjustment.

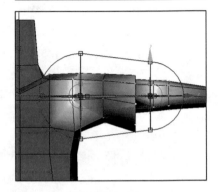

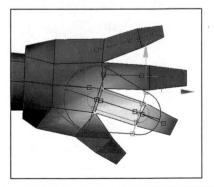

### Correct the Hand Envelopes

Now you can use the animation to help you spot problems with the skinning.

**Note:** The problems described in the rest of this section might not exactly match the problems you have with your own skinned character. But chances are, they will apply to some part of your character. You can apply these solutions to any part of the character as needed.

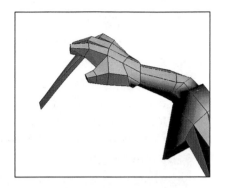

A common problem is the hand and finger envelopes not being large enough, so some vertices are not assigned to any bone. You will use the animation to spot and fix this problem if it has occurred with your mesh.

1. Scrub between frames 0 and 10.

2. Look for any parts of the hand or fingers that are left behind by the animation, and see if you can figure out which bone the vertices should belong to. Rotate the view as necessary to get a good look, and scrub to earlier frames if necessary to see where the mesh is pulling out.

   In the picture at right, the vertices that stayed behind belong to the last pinky link.

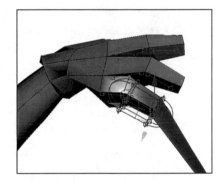

3. In the viewport or in the Parameters rollout, select the bone that the wayward part of the mesh should belong to.

4. Move one of the envelope handles away from the bone until the mesh snaps into place.

   You can also use the **Radius** parameter in the Envelope Properties group to increase the size of the cross section.

   If a small change to the cross section didn't fix the problem, then you've probably selected the wrong envelope or cross section. Undo your work and try again with a different cross section or envelope.

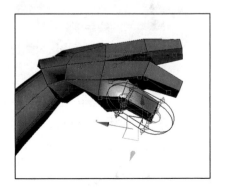

5. Look for other areas on the hands where the mesh doesn't follow the bones, and use the same procedure to fix the envelopes.

   Don't work on other parts of the body just yet. The goal now is simply to have all parts of the hands follow the hand and finger bones.

6. Save your work as **CharRig24.max**.

Parts of the mesh that stick out from the body, such as the shorts and shirt sleeves, probably don't follow along with the animation correctly. You will fix this by adjusting vertices manually.

### Weight the Pants

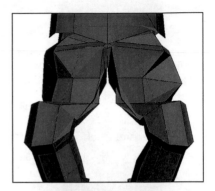

1. Continue with the scene from the previous exercise, or load *CharRig24.max* from the *Rigs* folder on the CD. If you load the file from the CD, select the body mesh and turn on **Edit Envelopes** on the **Modify** panel.

2. Go to frame 0.

3. In the Select group, check the **Vertices** checkbox, and uncheck **Cross Sections** and **Envelopes**.

4. In the Display rollout, check **Show No Envelopes**.

5. In the Front viewport, zoom in on the thighs.

6. In the Parameters rollout, select **BoneThighL**.

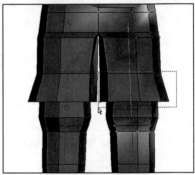

7. Draw a selection region around the vertices that make up the lower part of the shorts on the left leg. Each vertex is surrounded by a white box to indicate it is selected.

8. In the Weight Properties group, change the **Abs. Effect** parameter to 1.0.

   This assigns all the selected vertices to the left thigh bone. The mesh in that area turns red to indicate it receives all its influence from this bone.

9. Select **BoneThighR**, and select the vertices at the bottom of the right pant leg. Change **Abs. Effect** to 1.0.

   If you scrub the time slider, you will see that the bottoms of the pant legs now follow their respective thigh bones.

### Weight the Sleeves

You can use the same technique to make the shirt sleeves follow the arms.

1. Zoom into the left arm in the Front viewport.

2. In the Parameters rollout, select **BoneUpperArmL**.

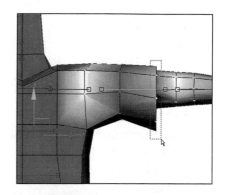

3. Draw a selection region around the vertices at the end of the sleeves to select them, and change **Abs. Effect** to **1.0**.

4. Pull the time slider to see the effect on the sleeves.

   The end of the sleeve moves with the arm as it should, but the sleeve vertices near the shoulder twist a little too much. You will fix this soon.

5. Do the same procedure you just performed on the right arm, selecting **BoneUpperArmR** and setting its end-of-sleeve vertices to an **Abs. Effect** value of **1.0**.

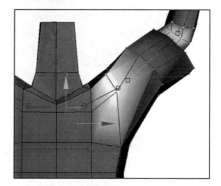

6. Save the scene as **CharRig25.max**.

### Create a Test Animation

By now, you've made all the easy, obvious corrections to the skinning. What remains is more vertex weighting at the joints. However, you won't be able to tell what needs correction unless you animate the rig to some degree.

Next, you will set up a short test animation with extreme poses. This will help you adjust the vertex weights and set up angle deformers where necessary.

1. Turn off **Edit Envelopes**.

2. Unhide the control objects and bones, and hide the body, head, and hair.

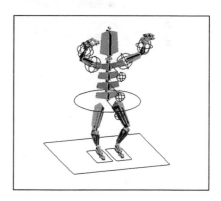

   Setting up the test animation with just the bones will keep you from becoming distracted by the incorrect mesh deformation.

3. Pull the time slider to see the current animation.

   If you have followed along with the book, your animation should show the character bending its knees and raising its arms at frame 10, then making a fist at frame 20.

4. Freeze the bones so you won't accidentally select them.

5. Turn on **Auto Key**.

6. On frame 20, move the wrist controls so the character's hands are by its sides. Rotate the wrist controls as necessary to pose the hands naturally, and rotate the clavicles downward slightly. You can also adjust the **ElbowSwivel** parameter, and curl or uncurl the fingers as you like.

    This gives you three poses for the arms: Straight out at the sides at frame 0, in the air at frame 10, and by the sides at frame 20.

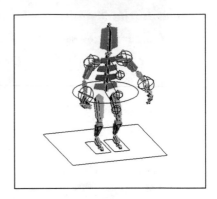

7. On frame 15, move the wrist controls away from the body to make the in-between pose more natural at that frame.

    You can also set a few poses for the feet to help you see how they deform as they roll off the ground.

8. On frame 10, move the left forward and the right foot back. Adjust **KneeSwivel** angles as you like.

9. On frame 15, animate each foot's **Roll** parameter to about **30**, then set each **Roll** parameter back to **0** on frames 10 and 20.

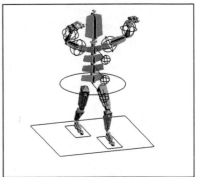

## Set Extreme Poses

To really test the skinning, you will need to put the character rig into a few different poses. Ideally, you would pose the character in the most extreme poses you expect it to make over the course of the animation.

You already have the arms moving up and down. Now you will animate the rest of the body in a series of poses that will allow you to see how the mesh is responding to the skinning process.

1. Select both foot controls, and right-click the time slider. On the Create Key dialog, click **OK**. This sets a key at frame 20 to keep the feet from moving until this frame.

2. Go to frame 30, and pose the body in a runner's position with the left leg in front, as shown in the picture at right. Rotate and move the foot controls and hand controls, and change the **KneeSwivel** and **ElbowSwivel** parameters as needed to make the pose as natural as possible.

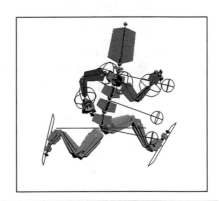

    Rotate the spine controls to make the character lean forward. You can also rotate the clavicles slightly to bend in the directions of the arms.

3. Go to frame 40 and reverse the pose, putting the right leg in front and the left in back. Reverse the arms and clavicles as well.

4. On frame 50, put the feet back on the ground, and rotate the spine backward and to the side to make the character lean back as an angle. Adjust the arms any way you like to suit the pose.

   This will help you see how the spine weights work when the character leans in different directions.

5. Pull the time slider to see how the animation is coming along.

   Keep in mind that you are not trying to accurately animate the character running. You are simply setting a few poses to help you with the skinning. Even so, it's helpful during the weighting process to have the character moving smoothly from one pose to the next.

   The arms and legs are drawn into the body on frame 35. Let's make that transition pose smoother.

6. On frame 35, move the feet near the ground, and move the wrists downward.

   When you scrub the time slider, the body should move smoothly from one pose to the next.

   Next, you will move the body control. This will help you test that all vertices are moving with the body.

7. On frame 10, use the Front viewport to move **CtrlBody** to the left, a short distance from its original position.

   Our test animation is now complete.

8. Turn off **Auto Key**, and save the scene as **CharRig26.max**.

   If you have trouble creating this animation, load the file *CharRig26.max* from the *Rigs* folder on the CD, and look at the animation in the file.

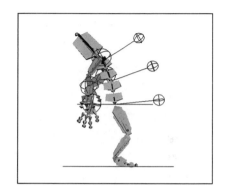

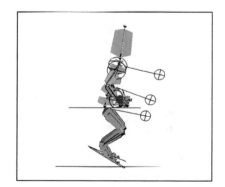

### Look for Wayward Vertices

Now you can use the animation to help you find vertices that need correction. The first step is to find vertices that have no weighting at all, so you can make them follow the body.

1. Unhide the body mesh, and hide the bones and control objects.

2. Pull the time slider between frames 0 and 10.

   If any vertices stay behind when **CtrlBody** moves to the side, this means the vertices aren't assigned to any bone at all. You'll weight these manually.

### Fix Wayward Vertices

1. Select the body mesh., and turn on **Edit Envelopes**.

2. Pull the time slider back and forth to identify a vertex or group of vertices that are not moving with the body.

3. On any frame, select a vertex or group of vertices that should all move with the same bone.

4. In the Parameters rollout, highlight the bone that the vertices should move with.

   If you're not sure which bone to select, take a guess. You can always fine-tune the vertex weights later.

5. Pull the time slider to frame 10.

6. Set **Abs. Effect** to **1.0**.

   The vertices will snap to the mesh.

7. Repeat this process for every wayward vertex.

   This ensures that every vertex on the body is assigned to at least one bone, and you won't be distracted by wayward vertices as you weight the rest of the body.

8. Save the scene as **CharRig27.max**.

### ☼ TIP ☼

*It's easiest to select the wayward vertices on a frame later than 0, since they're out in space away from the body.*

## Weight the Left Foot

So far, you have used manual weighting to make specific vertices follow one bone only. Now it's time to start weighting the vertices that follow two or three different bones.

This is where the real work begins. The first time you perform these tasks, you might find that you make a mess of things. If that happens, just go to frame 0, select the vertices that are giving you trouble, and weight them back to 1.0 on one bone or another.

We'll start with the feet and ankles, since these vertices need to be weighted on two bones only. Your first task is to set up some working weights that will provide a good foundation for the rest of the foot weighting.

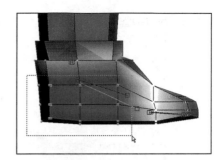

For starters, the heel should be weighted completely to the foot bone, and the tips of the toes should be weighted to the toe bone. The area at the ball of the foot where it bends should be weighted halfway between the two.

You'll weight the left foot only for now, and mirror the settings to the other side of the body later on.

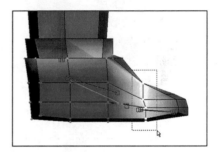

1. Go to frame 10.

2. In the Left viewport, zoom in on the left foot, the foot posed in the front.

3. Select the vertices at the heel and middle part of the foot.

4. Select **BoneFootL**, and change **Abs. Effect** to 1.0.

5. Select the vertices at the ball of the foot, and set **Abs. Effect** to 0.5.

6. Select **BoneToeL**, and set **Abs. Effect** to 0.5.

7. Select the vertices at the toe, and set **Abs. Effect** to 1.0.

   This gives you a starting point for weighting the vertices at the ball of the foot.

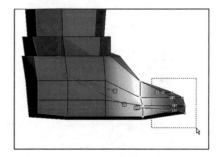

## Adjust the Foot Weights

1. Pull the time slider to frame 15.

   As you watch the animation, ignore the way the ankle looks. You should concern yourself only with the ball of the foot for now.

---

☀ **TIP** ☀

*A character rigger must develop the ability to look at one part of the body while ignoring problems in other parts of the body.*

If the ball of the foot slides when the heel comes up, then the vertices at the bottom of the ball will need to be fully weighted to the toe.

2. Select the vertices at the bottom of the ball of the foot.

3. Make sure **BoneToeL** is selected, and set **Abs. Effect** to 1.0.

### Adjust the Ankle

Next, you will need to use your judgment to adjust the ankle weights. Let's set up some weights for the foot and calf as a starting point.

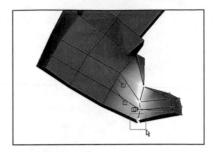

1. Go to frame 10.

2. Select all the vertices at the left ankle.

3. For both **BoneCalfL** and **BoneFootL**, set **Abs. Effect** to **0.5**.

4. Pull the time slider to watch the animation. Look for the frame where the angle between the calf and foot bones is most severe, such as frame 25 or 30.

   At this extreme angle, you can see whether the ankle bends too much or too little. In the picture at right, the top row of ankle vertices follows the foot too much, making the bend look rubbery.

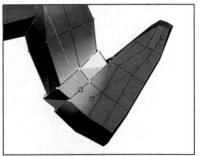

   To fix the bend, you'll work with one row of vertices at a time.

5. Go to frame 10, and select the topmost row of vertices in the ankle.

6. Pull the time slider to the frame where ankle bend is the most severe.

7. While watching the viewport, use the **Abs. Effect** spinner to gradually increase or decrease this value until the selected vertices follow the calf bone more than the foot bone.

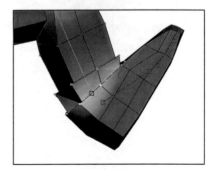

   It doesn't matter whether you have **BoneCalfL** or **BoneFootL** currently selected. Changing the **Abs. Effect** for one of these bones will automatically change it for the other. For example, if you increase the **Abs. Effect** value for **BoneCalfL**, it will automatically reduce for **BoneFootL**. The selected vertices' weights for both bones will always add up to 1.0.

8. Go to frame 10, and select the next row of vertices on the ankle. Go to a frame where the angle is severe, and adjust the **Abs. Effect** value as necessary.

   If your character has more rows of vertices at the ankle, continue doing this for each row of vertices until the ankle bend looks as natural as possible.

**Weight the Left Knee**

You will use the same process to weight the left knee's vertices.

1. Go to frame 0.

2. In the Front viewport, select all the vertices at the left knee, including the last row of vertices on the pant leg.

3. For **BoneCalfL** and **BoneThighL**, set **Abs. Effect** to 0.5.

4. Select the topmost row of vertices on the knee (the lowest vertices on the pant leg), and pull the time slider to a frame where the knee bend is severe.

5. Adjust the **Abs. Effect** value until the knee looks better.

6. Do the same for each row of vertices, selecting them on frame 0 and adjusting **Abs. Effect** on a frame where the knee is bent to see how the mesh responds.

   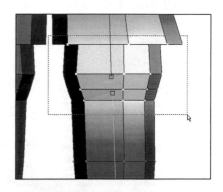
   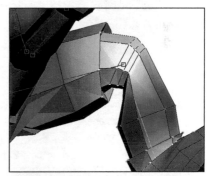

   Using this technique, you'll be able to make a big improvement to the way mesh deforms, but the knee will still lose some of its volume as it bends. In addition, the shorts might pass through the leg as it passes behind the body around frame 35.

   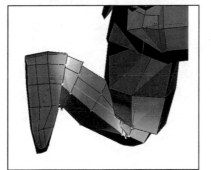
   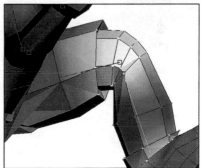

   You can fix these problems with a joint angle deformer. You will use this tool in a later tutorial to prevent the knee from losing volume, and to prevent the shorts from passing through the leg.

7. Save the scene as **CharRig28.max**.

## SKIN MIRROR MODE

A new skinning tool in 3ds max 6, Mirror Mode, allows you to paste envelope settings and vertex weights from one side of the character's body to the other.

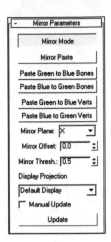

To use this tool, you must first access the Skin Modifier's Envelope sub-object level. Then you can turn on Mirror Mode on the Mirror Parameters rollout.

To mirror the settings, select vertices on the mesh for which envelopes and vertex weights have already been set up. Then increase the Mirror Thresh value until the selected vertices turn yellow, and the corresponding vertices on the opposite side of the body turn green (on the right side) or blue (on the left side).

When the vertices are the appropriate colors, click Mirror Paste to paste all envelope and vertex settings from the yellow side to the opposite side.

### Tutorial S4: MIRRORING ENVELOPES AND VERTEX WEIGHTS

1. Continue with the file you created in the last tutorial, or load the file *CharRig28.max* from the *Rigs* folder on the CD. If you load the file, select the body mesh and go to the **Envelope** sub-object level for the **Skin** modifier.

2. In the Parameters rollout under the Select group, make sure **Vertices** is checked.

3. In the Mirror Parameters rollout, click **Mirror Mode** to turn it on.

4. In the Front viewport, select all the vertices on the character's left side. This is the side of the character that's on your right when viewed in the Front viewport. Do not select the vertices down the center of the character.

    Some of the vertices on the left side turn yellow to indicate they are selected, while some of the vertices on the right turn green. Many are still red, indicating they will not be affected by the mirroring operation in their current state.

☀ **TIP** ☀

*Skin Mirror Mode works best when the mesh's pivot point is at the center of the mesh, and is aligned with the world. If you followed the instructions in this book, your character is already set up this way.*

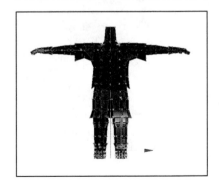

**Mirror Mode** operates over a specific distance from the mesh's pivot point. This distance is set by the **Mirror Thresh** value. You will increase this value to include all the vertices in the mirroring operation.

5. Watch the character in the Front viewport while increasing the **Mirror Thresh** value. Vertices on the character's left side will turn from red to yellow as you change this value, while vertices on the right will change from red to green. Increase **Mirror Thresh** until the vertices stop changing color.

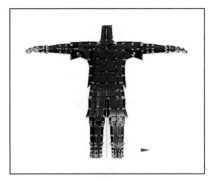

   When the vertices stop changing colors, this means you have increased the **Mirror Thresh** value enough to include all the vertices in the mesh.

6. Click **Mirror Paste**.

   This pastes the envelope and vertex settings from the selected side (left) to the opposite side (right).

7. Turn off **Mirror Mode**.

   The changes you made to the left side of the body are pasted to the right side. Test the changes by pulling the time slider to see how the right foot reacts to the animation.

   If the right foot doesn't deform correctly, the most likely cause is that you didn't increase the **Mirror Thresh** value high enough before pasting. Select the left side vertices and try again.

| ☀ TIP ☀ |
| --- |
| *You can also use Mirror Mode on just a small selection of vertices, such as an arm or hand.* |

8. Save the scene as **CharRig29.max**.

# Tutorial S5: Customizing Joints with the Joint Angle Deformer

The joint angle deformer is ideal for joints that bend on one axis only, such as knees and elbows. This skinning tool allows you to customize the way vertices deform at joints by moving the vertices into place.

## Apply the Joint Angle Deformer

You apply a joint angle deformer to the child object of the bone pair. Since you will apply it to the knee, the child bone is the calf. We'll start by applying the deformer to the left knee.

1. Continue with the file you created in the last tutorial, or load the file *CharRig28.max* from the *Rigs* folder on the CD. If you load the file, select the body mesh and go to the **Envelope** sub-object level for the **Skin** modifier.

2. In the Parameters rollout, select **BoneCalfL**.

3. Go to frame 0.

4. In the Front viewport, select the vertices at the knee, including one or two rows of vertices above and below the knee.

5. In the Gizmos rollout, make sure *Joint Angle Deformer* is selected from the dropdown menu, and click **Add Gizmo**.

   The joint angle deformer gizmo appears around the selected vertices.

6. In the Gizmo Parameters rollout, click **Edit Lattice**.

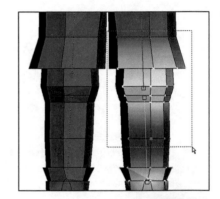

## Adjust the Joint Angle Deformer

Adjusting the joint angle deformer's lattice can be tricky when the character's body is animated. When you go to a frame where the joint is bent, the lattice might not be in alignment with the Left viewport.

To make it easier to adjust the lattice, you will use the User viewport and the Screen coordinate system.

1. Go to a frame at which the knee bend reaches its peak in front of the body, such as frame 29 or 30.

2. In the User viewport, zoom in on the knee.

3. Use **Arc Rotate** to rotate the User view so you have a side view of the lattice, where points on both sides of the lattice are lined up with one another in the viewport.

4. Click **Select and Move**.

5. Choose the **Screen** coordinate system.

   This coordinate system sets the XY plane to match the current actively viewport, even when the User viewport is active. This means you can move the vertices in the User viewport on the X and Y axes, and the vertices will move where expected rather than shooting off into space as they do with the View coordinate system.

<table>
<tr><td>

≗ **TIP** ≗

The default coordinate system, View, is actually a combination of the Screen and World coordinate systems. View uses the World system in User and Perspective viewports, and the Screen system in all other viewports such as Top, Front, and Left.

</td></tr>
</table>

6. Adjust the points on the lattice to give the knee more volume.

7. Go to the frame where the pants cut through the legs most severely. Rotate the User view so you have a straight view of the lattice, and adjust the points accordingly.

8. Scrub the time slider and watch the knee deform over the course of the animation, and make any corrections as necessary.

   If you find that the lattice "pops" or jiggles too much, click **Edit Angle Keys Curves** on the Gizmo Parameters rollout. Scrub the animation while watching the Joint Graph, and see if any of your angle keys are too close together. If they are, select the offending keys and delete them, or move them to match other keys at a nearby angle. When you have finished, close the Joint Graph.

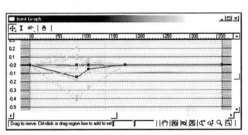

9. Turn off **Edit Lattice**, and save the scene as **CharRig30.max**.

   The left knee and foot are now correctly skinned.

   You can apply the same tools to the right leg to skin it the same way. If you do so, save your scene as **CharRig31.max**. Alternately, you can load this file from the *Rigs* folder on the CD.

The hips and shoulders are the most difficult parts of a character to skin correctly. Each part of the hip is affected by both the spine and at least one thigh bone. Some vertices, such as those at the center of the hips, are affected by both thigh bones as well as the spine. You also have the added challenge of a t-shirt that hangs below the waist.

**☼ TIP ☼**

*Some riggers create their rigs with a small bone at the top of each thigh that doesn't affect any vertices, but simply provides a parent bone for an angle deformer.*

With this particular rig, you can't use a joint angle deformer on the thighs because they have no parent bone in the skin system. Recall that the thighs are linked to the control object **CtrlLegs** rather than another bone.

You might be tempted to weight one side and use **Mirror Mode** to pass the settings to the other side. But because most parts of the hips are affected by both thigh bones, this isn't a very useful solution.

Instead, you will adjust the skinning at the hips with plain old vertex weighting. Let's start by setting some basic weights as a starting point.

**☼ TIP ☼**

*There's no magic secret to weighting on multiple bones–you just have to get in there and do it. The only way to learn this skill is with practice.*

### Weight the Hips

1. Continue with the file you created in the previous tutorial, or load the file *CharRig31.max* from the *Rigs* folder on the CD. If you load the file, select the body mesh, go to the **Modify** panel, and turn on **Edit Envelopes** for the **Skin** modifier.

2. Go to frame 0.

3. In the Front viewport, select the vertices at the hips, including the vertices at the creases of the thighs. Select **BoneSpine01**, and set **Abs. Effect** to 1.0.

4. Select **BoneThighL**.

5. Working your way down the character's left side, select three or four vertices at a time on that side of the character, and set weights as follows:

   - Near the waist: **0.2**
   - Shirttail: **0.4**
   - Hip below shirttail: **0.6**
   - Crease at thighs: **0.8**
   - Center crotch area: **0.4**

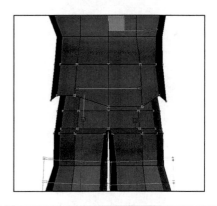

6 Select **BoneThighR**, and do the same for the vertices on the character's right side.

### Fine-Tune the Vertex Weights

Now you can start fine-tuning the weights. This process must be done on one or two vertices at a time. You'll start the process on a frame where the thighs don't bend much.

1. Pull the time slider to frame 15 or 20.

2. Use **Arc Rotate** to look at the hips from all angles.

3. When you see a vertex that isn't deforming correctly, select the appropriate thigh bone, select the vertex, and use the **Abs. Effect** spinner to increase or decrease the bone's influence over the vertex.

   In addition to adjusting the vertex weights on each individual thigh, you will find that the hips deform more smoothly if you make each thigh affect the vertices in the opposite thigh's crease by a very small amount, such as 0.1.

4. Pull the time slider between frames 15 and 20 to see the effects of your changes.

5. When you think you've done a decent job of weighting at these frames, pull the time slider to frame 30 to look at the first extreme pose.

   Don't be concerned if the pants go through the shirt at frame 30. The leg won't be posed like this very often in the final animation, and when it is, the pants will hide the shirt from view.

6. Rotate around the User view, and adjust the thigh and hip vertices as necessary.

   The buttock and crotch areas are the trickiest ones to adjust. Select one vertex at a time, and experiment with different weight settings for each thigh, and for **BoneSpine01**. Scrub the time slider between frames 30 and 40 to make sure the vertices at the center of the buttocks are responding correctly.

   It's perfectly fine to have a crease at the thigh in the extreme poses. In fact, this is desirable, since it mimics the way clothing responds when you bend your leg by more than 30 degrees or so.

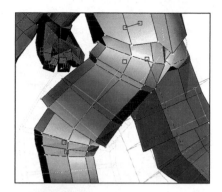

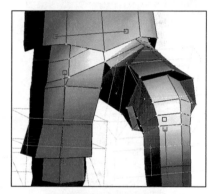

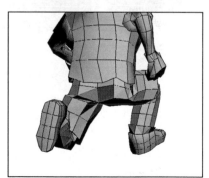

If something strange is happening with the vertices and you can't figure out what it is, it's possible the vertices are being influenced by another bone that you don't know about.

To find out which bones are influencing a vertex or set of vertices, you can use the *weight table*. The weight table is a chart that lists all vertices and all bones, and shows you the weights for each one.

7. In the Weight Properties group, click **Weight Table**. At the lower left of the Weight Table dialog, choose *Selected Vertices* from the dropdown menu.

You can scroll the display to the left or right to see which bones affect the selected vertices. The weight for each bone that affects the vertices is listed under that bone on the chart.

If a vertex is being affected by a bone when it shouldn't, you can change its weight right on the chart. You can type a value into the chart, or drag to the left or right on the value itself.

8. When you are satisfied with the hip weights, save the scene as **CharRig32.max**.

## Check Your Work with MeshSmooth

Congratulations! You're more than halfway through the weighting process. Take a moment to pat yourself on the back, then get back to work.

It can be very satisfying to see the mesh when it's all smoothed out, so let's see how the **MeshSmooth** modifier looks with the skinning so far.

1. Apply the **MeshSmooth** modifier to the body.

2. Set **Iterations** to 1.

3. Rotate the User viewport to see the model from all angles.

4. After you've had a good look, turn off the **MeshSmooth** modifier temporarily by clicking the light bulb next to the modifier name.

<table>
<tr><td>☼ TIP ☼</td></tr>
<tr><td>I find the weight table most useful after I've already adjusted most of the vertex weights manually, but there are still a few that are misbehaving. It's especially useful for adjusting the vertices down the center of the hips, which are influenced by three different bones. Use the weight table to help you figure out how the three weights should work together.</td></tr>
</table>

## Weight the Rest of the Character

From this point, it's just a matter of using the tools you already know to finish up the skinning.

1. On frame 15, zoom in on the shoulders. Use the animation between frames 15 and 20 to adjust the vertex weights at the shoulder. You can adjust the weights at frame 15, then scrub to frame 20 to see how the weights work with a different pose.

Vertices at the upper arm can be weighted to the upper arm, clavicle, or topmost spine bone. Be sure to do both arms, and use **Arc Rotate** to check the weighting at the back of the model as well as the front.

You can also check the arms at frames 20 through 40 to be sure your weights work reasonably well throughout the animation. It's normal for the arms to look a little boxy.

If you like, you can weight one shoulder and mirror the settings to the other side using **Mirror Mode**.

2. Look over the spine and neck to see if their vertex weights require any correction. The top of the neck nub should be weighted 100% to **BoneHead**. If you like, you can unhide the head to make sure the neck nub stays inside it at all times.

3. Check the wrists and elbows to see if they deform properly, and make adjustments to vertex weights as necessary. If you like, you can use a joint angle deformer on the elbows to prevent them from losing volume when they bend.

4. Check the fingers to make sure they're weighted correctly. An easy way to check them is to unhide **CtrlWristR** and **CtrlWristL** and change the finger curl attributes while watching the fingers onscreen. Make adjustments to vertex weights as necessary.

That's all there is to it. It takes time, but your reward is a character that animates smoothly.

> ☝ **TIP** ☝
>
> *Don't be concerned if the shoulders twist a little when the arm rises. This will not be very noticeable once the model is smoothed.*

> ☝ **TIP** ☝
>
> *Professional riggers sometimes spend several days adjusting vertex weights, so don't be surprised if your first try takes a few hours.*

5. For a final check, turn on the **MeshSmooth** modifier and pull the time slider to see how the body deforms throughout the animation.

6. Save your work as **CharRig33.max**.

**Prepare the Rig for Animation**

The last step in rigging and skinning a character is to prepare the scene for animation.

1. Hide all parts of the mesh.

2. Unhide the bones, and freeze them

3. Unhide the control objects.

3. Turn on **Auto Key**.

4. On frame 0, move and rotate the wrist controls to place the character's hands at its sides.

5. Select all the control objects, and delete all their keys from the Trackbar.

    Your rig is now ready to be animated.

6. Save the scene as **CharRigFinal.max**.

    Now you're ready to use the fruits of your labor in practice. Continue on to the *Character Animation* chapter to bring the character to life.

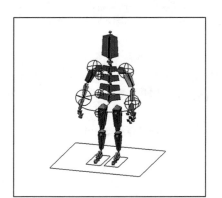

# 4

# CHARACTER ANIMATION

*Character animation* brings a character to life
using principles borrowed from traditional animation.

Animating a character is one of the most rewarding and entertaining things you can do with 3ds max. Your enjoyment of the process will increase as you learn more about how it's done.

Computer-generated character animation has its roots in hand-drawn animation, with rules and principles developed in the first half of the 1900's. The approach, techniques, and terms you will use while animating with 3ds max all come from this traditional field.

This chapter will not attempt to teach you everything there is to know about character animation. There are numerous books and other learning materials that already cover this subject in great detail. The purpose of this chapter is to introduce you to the most important concepts, and to show you how to use 3ds max to animate your own characters.

One of the primary tools an animator has is his or her own body. When trying to figure out how to animate a particular motion or facial expression, your first course of action should be to do it yourself.

For body motions, you can do the motion slowly at first to see how your torso bends or leans, and how your limbs move. Then do the motions at normal speed to get a feel for the timing.

For facial expressions, your best tool is a mirror. Make the faces yourself, and note how your facial muscles and features respond to each emotion.

Professional animators use these tools daily. Be sure to use them yourself!

## TOOLS IN 3DS MAX

3ds max has a number of tools designed for creating and editing animation.

### KEYS

Creating a basic animation with 3ds max is easy—you turn on Auto Key, move the time slider to a frame later than zero, and move, rotate or scale objects.

Each time you do so, 3ds max creates a *key* at the current frame. That frame then becomes a *keyframe*. When you play the animation, 3ds max figures out the action in between the keyframes. In other words, 3ds max *interpolates* the animation between keys.

There are a number of tools in 3ds max that you can use to set and change keys, and to change the way the animation interpolates between keys. Your primary tools for working with keys are the Trackbar, and the Track View windows.

### TRACKBAR

The Trackbar is located below the time slider. When you create a key, a red rectangle appears on the Trackbar at that frame number to indicate that there's a key there. It doesn't tell you whether it's a position, rotation, or scale key, or whether one of the object's parameters has been animated. It simply tells you that there's a key of some kind at that frame.

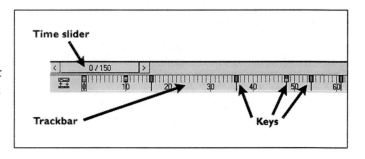

The Trackbar also shows the active time segment, which is the number of frames currently available in the animation. You can change the active time segment by clicking Time Configuration at the lower right of the screen and changing the Length parameter on the Time Configuration dialog.

The Trackbar is useful for simple edits such as moving or copying keys to change the animation's timing.

In the next tutorial, you will learn to use the Trackbar to copy and edit keys. If you already know how to use the Trackbar, you can skip to the next tutorial.

# Tutorial A1: Working with Keys

In this tutorial, you'll animate a character making a few simple motions. You'll also adjust the animation using the Trackbar and other keyframing tools.

## Animate a Waving Arm

1. Load the file *CharAnimRig.max* from the *Animation/Scenes* folder on the CD, or load the character rig you saved at the end of the *Skinning* chapter.

   This scene contains a character rig, ready to be animated. You can animate the character by moving and rotating the controls at the shoulders, wrists, spine, and feet. The bones have been frozen so you won't select them by accident.

   **Note:** If you're using a rig you created yourself (rather than the one from the CD), link the wrist controls to **CtrlLegs** before continuing. This setup will be more appropriate for this practice exercise.

   When posing the arm and hand for a waving motion, they will look very strange at first. You must keep the final goal in mind, and follow through with all the steps to complete the pose.

2. Turn on **Auto Key**.

3. Go to frame 10.

   You can get to frame 10 by pulling the time slider, or by entering the number 10 in the frame number entry area at the lower right of the screen. If you enter the frame number manually, be sure to press **[Enter]** after typing it.

4. In the Front viewport, raise right wrist control so it's at roughly the same height as the character's neck.

   This will make the elbow and hand look very strange. Don't worry, just keep going!

5. Click **Select and Rotate**, and choose the **Local** coordinate system.

6. Rotate the wrist control until the palm faces away from the character, as if it were waving hello.

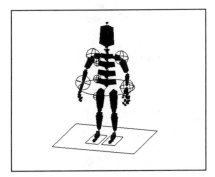

## ☙ TIP ☙

If you didn't do the rigging tutorials, take a few moments to play with the controls and get a feel for what they do. Before continuing with this exercise, be sure to undo any movements or rotations you make, or reload the file *CharAnimRig.max*.

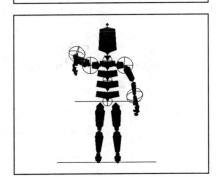

## ☙ TIP ☙

It will be easier for you to rotate the control objects if you use the Local coordinate system, because the rotation gizmo will always correspond to the hand's orientation.

7. On the **Modify** panel, adjust the **ElbowSwivel** parameter to bring the elbow into a natural pose for waving the arm.

8. In the Top viewport, move the wrist control in front of the body a little to make the pose more natural.

## Lower the Hand

On frame 20, you want the character to put its hand back by its side. There is already a key for this pose on frame 0, so you'll simply copy the key from frame 0 to 20.

1. Go to frame 20.

2. Select the right wrist control, if it's not already selected.

3. On the Trackbar, select the key at frame 0 by clicking it. The key turns white to indicate that it's selected.

4. Hold down **[Shift]**, and move the key from frame 0 to 20.

The character's wrist returns to its rest position.

## Adjust Intermediate Frames

1. Scrub (pull) the time slider back and forth between frames 0 and 20.

3ds max has interpolated the frames between 0 and 10, and 10 and 20. To do this, 3ds max takes the shortest path between the two different rotational values for the wrist controls. This often yields results that require you to make adjustments at intermediate frames.

2. Go to frame 5.

3. In the Top viewport, move the hand farther in front of the body.

4. Rotate the wrist control so the palm faces the ground.

This intermediate pose is more in line with the way your hand moves naturally when coming up for a wave.

5. Copy the key from frame 5 to frame 15 by holding down **[Shift]** and moving the key.

6. Scrub the time slider between frames 0 and 20.

The waving motion now looks more natural.

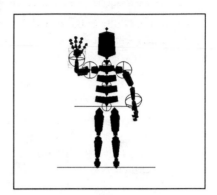

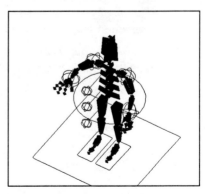

---

**TIP**

*In the context of 3D animation, the term "scrub" means to move back and forth in time to see the animation. You can do this by pulling the time slider back and forth.*

---

## Wave the Left Arm

Now we want the character to wave its other arm.

1. Go to frame 30.

2. Move and rotate the character's left wrist control to make the left arm wave hello.

3. Pull the time slider between frames 0 and 30 to see the animation.

There's a problem here. The left arm starts moving at frame 0, rather than staying still until frame 20. This is because the program is interpolating between the only two keys you've set for this object, at frames 0 and 30.

The real problem is that there's no key at frame 20. To solve this problem, you can copy the left wrist key from frame 0 to 20. When 3ds max interpolates between these keys, there will be no in-between motion because the keys will be exactly the same.

4. Hold down **[Shift]**, and copy the key at frame 0 to frame 20.

5. Pull the time slider again. The character's left arm stays still until frame 20, then starts moving.

The problem you just solved is a common one when animating with 3ds max. The program simply interpolates from one key to the next. If there is no key, it places one at frame 0 and interpolates from there. If you want a body part to stay still for a certain period of time, you must set a key to tell it to do so.

Let's copy another key to make the arm come back down at frame 40.

6. Copy the key at frame 20 to frame 40.

7. On frame 25, adjust the left arm to a more natural intermediate pose, and copy this key to frame 35.

8. Play the animation.

Now the character raises its right arm and puts it down, then raises its left arm and puts it down.

9. Save the scene as **CharAnimWave01.max**.

### Bend the Knees

Next, you'll make the character bend its knees.

To bend the knees, you can simply select **CtrlLegs** (the circle around the hips) and move it downward. But suppose you want the character to keep its knees straight until frame 40, then bend its knees at frame 50. You'll need to set a key for **CtrlLegs** at frame 40 to keep it from moving until that point.

You have already learned how to copy a key from one frame to another by holding down **[Shift]** and moving the key on the Trackbar. Let's try a different method for copying keys.

1. Select **CtrlLegs**, the circle at the hips.

2. At any frame, right-click the time slider.

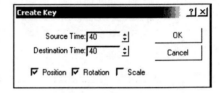

   The Create Key dialog appears. You will only ever animate the position and rotation of your control objects, so you only have to copy these keys.

3. In the Create Key dialog, leave **Position** and **Rotation** turned on, and turn off **Scale**.

4. Set the **Source Time** and **Destination Time** to **40**, and click **OK**.

   This sets a key for **CtrlLegs** at frame 40. There's no key at frame 0, which is just fine.

5. Go to frame 50.

6. In the Front viewport, move **CtrlLegs** downward to bend the knees.

   Now you want the character to come back up on frame 60.

7. Copy the key at frame 40 to frame 60 using either of the methods you now know.

8. Play the animation.

   After raising each arm, the character bends its knees, then stands up again.

9. Save the scene as **CharAnimWave02.max**.

## WALK CYCLE

A *walk cycle* is exactly that: A cycle of motion for making a character walk. It's called a *cycle* because it can be repeated over and over again. The walk cycle is part of any professional character animator's bag of tricks.

Before you animate a walk cycle, get up and study how you actually walk. Use this guide to help you figure out what a walk is made of:

- Start from a standing position, with your feet under your shoulders.

- If you want to start walking, what's the first thing you do?

- How far do you place your stepping foot from the one behind?

- What is the foot in the back doing while you step?

- Does the foot in front bend? How about the back foot?

- Are your knees bent or straight?

- Are you taller when one foot is in the air, or when both feet are on the ground?

- What are your hips doing while you walk? It can be helpful to put a hand on the side of one hip and see if you can feel any shifts as you move.

- Now swing your arms a little while you walk. Do they match your legs, or do they move opposite your legs?

- What do your shoulders do as you swing your arms?

The answers to these questions will help you animate a walk cycle more effectively.

> ### ☕ TIP ☕
>
> *Walking is so natural for most of us that it can be hard to determine what your body is doing. You can get a better feel for what's actually going on by exaggerating your motions a little bit.*

## THE SET KEY SYSTEM

When animating a walk cycle, you'll be setting keys for many parts of the rig at regular intervals. It would be very tedious if you had to keep checking to see where the last key was set for each body part, and had to keep copying keys to keep body parts from moving.

An alternate tool for setting keys is the Set Key system. With this system, you can set (create) a key for several objects with just one mouse click. This saves you the trouble of going back later and copying keys to keep objects from moving. The Set Key system is ideal for setting up cycles of motion, such as a walk cycle.

The controls used in the Set Key system are located at the lower right of the screen, just below the end of the Trackbar. Before using the Set Key system, you will need to create a selection set that includes all the objects for which you want to set keys. In addition, you must use the Key Filters tool to specify the tracks for which you want to set keys.

Set Key When the Set Key button is turned on, you can click Set Keys (the button

 with the image of a key on it) to set keys for filtered tracks on objects in the selection set at that frame.

The Set Key system is particularly useful for roughing out an animation sequence. For example, animators often rough out a scene by setting keys at regular intervals, such as every 5 or 10 frames. The Set Key system makes this process very fast.

Afterward, the animator moves or deletes keys to adjust the timing. For that task, the Auto Key system described earlier works better.

> ### ☺ TIP ☺
> A track is a holder for a linear series of information, such as a series of keys for an object. In 3ds max, each object has several animation tracks, one for each parameter that can be animated. For example, a box object would have tracks for Position, Rotation, and Scale, as well as Length, Height, Width, and other animatable parameters.

> ### ☺ TIP ☺
> Animators use the term "roughing out" to describe the process of quickly placing keys at approximate times. The result, a "rough sequence," gives the animator an idea of how the motion will flow, and provides the basis for the final animation.

## Tutorial A2: Creating a Walk Cycle

Before you start animating a walk cycle, you'll take a look at a completed walk cycle to see how it's keyframed.

### Load a Completed Walk Cycle

1. Load the file *CharAnimWalk.max* from the *Animation/Scenes* folder on the CD.

   This scene contains an example of a walk cycle.

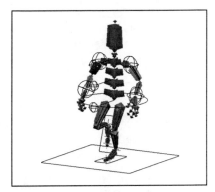

2. Play the animation.

   The character walks forward slowly, taking a step on each foot. Its final pose is the same as its starting pose, but in a different location in the scene.

   In this animation, the keys have been set every 10 frames. Let's take a closer look at the keyframes.

3. Go to frame 0, and study the pose.

   The character has one foot in the air, and is standing nearly straight.

4. Scrub the time slider slowly from frame 0 to frame 10.

   The character puts its right foot forward, just barely reaching the ground as it leans forward.

5. Scrub the time slider to frame 20.

   The character shifts its weight from the back foot to the front foot.

6. Scrub the time slider to frame 30.

   The character is posed in a mirror image of the pose at frame 0, this time with its left foot in the air.

7. Scrub the time slider to frame 60.

   The character repeats the same motions with the other foot.

8. Now play the animation while watching it in the Front viewport.

   As the character steps onto one leg, it shifts its weight from one side to the other.

   Now you're ready to animate your own walk cycle using the Set Key system.

## Prepare the Scene for Set Key

1. Load *CharAnimWalkLegs01.max* from the *Animation/Scenes* folder on the CD.

    This file contains a simplified rig to make it easier for you to practice making a walk cycle. The rig is posed at frame 0 in the *passing position*, where one foot is in the air, ready to take a step.

    To use the Set Key system, you will need a selection set that includes all objects for which you want to set keys. This would be all the control objects. This selection set, called *Control Objects*, already exists.

2. At the lower right of the screen, just above the **Key Filters** button, choose the selection set *Control Objects* from the list.

    Now you must indicate the tracks within those objects for which you want to set keys.

3. Click **Key Filters**. In the Set Key Filters dialog, turn on **Position**, **Rotation**, and **Custom Attributes**, and turn off all other options. Close the dialog by clicking the **[X]** at its upper right corner.

 4. Turn on the **Set Key** button. The button turns red to indicate it is turned on.

5. Go to frame 0.

 6. Click **Set Keys** (the large button with the image of a key).

    This sets a key for all the control objects at the current frame.

## Animate the First Leg Pose

Now you can start animating the legs to make the character walk.

1. Go to frame 10.

2. In Left viewport, move **CtrlLegs** (the circle at the hips) down and to the right, and rotate it slightly to make the character lean forward.

    The rig will look strange while you're posing it. This is normal.

3. Move and rotate the right foot control to pose the character in a stepping motion.

4. Click **Set Keys**.

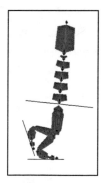 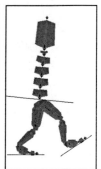

---

## Animate the Stepping Pose

Animating the rest of the walk cycle is as simple as creating more poses and setting keys for them.

1. Go to frame 20.

2. In the Left viewport, move **CtrlLegs** slightly up and to the right.

3. Rotate the right foot to step flat on the ground, and move it so it's at the same height as the left foot.

4. Select **CtrlFootL**. On the **Modify** panel, in the Custom Attributes rollout, set **Roll** to **90**.

5. Click **Set Keys**.

## Animate the Passing Position

1. Go to frame 30.

2. In the Left viewport, move **CtrlLegs** up and to the right, so the right leg is nearly straight. Rotate it to make the character stand up straight.

3. Select **CtrlFootL**. Change the **Roll** parameter to 0, and move and rotate the foot into the passing position.

   The result of changing the **Roll** parameter might not update until you click **Set Keys**.

4. Click **Set Keys**.

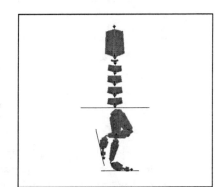

5. Scrub the time slider between frames 0 and 30 to see the animation so far. If the animation looks wrong, look back over the steps to see which pose is incorrect. Fix the pose, and click **Set Keys**.

   If the back leg appears to straighten then jerk forward around frame 20, you can move **CtrlLegs** down a little on frame 20 to bend the knees more. Be sure to click **Set Keys** after making this change.

## Animate the Remaining Poses

The rest of the walk is a repeat of the first part, but with the left leg stepping forward instead of the right. Use the pictures on the next page as a guide when setting the remainder of the poses.

1. Go to frame 40. Move and rotate the left foot in the stepping position. Move **CtrlLegs** forward slightly, and rotate it to make the character lean forward. Click **Set Keys**.

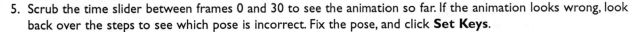

2. On frame 50, set the left foot flat on the ground and move **CtrlLegs** slightly forward and up. For **CtrlFootR**, change Roll to 90. Click **Set Keys**.

3. On frame 60, bring the right foot up into the passing position and set **Roll** back to 0. Move **CtrlLegs** to straighten out the right leg, and rotate it to straighten up the spine. Click **Set Keys**.

4. Scrub the time slider between frames 0 and 60 to see the animation.

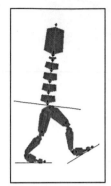  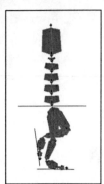

**Balance the Character**

The walk is coming along. But if you watch the animation in the Front viewport, you will see that the character isn't balanced. When it's on one leg, its entire weight should be centered over the standing leg.

1. Go to frame 0. In the Front viewport, move **CtrlLegs** to the right to center the spine over the left leg. Click **Set Keys**.

On frame 10, the character is about to place its foot on the ground. Here, its weight is almost centered over the two legs, but not quite.

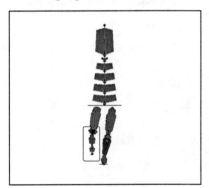

3. On frame 10, in the Front viewport, move **CtrlLegs** slightly to the right, and click **Set Keys**.

On frames 20 and 50, the character's weight is balanced between both legs. This is appropriate for this pose because both feet are on the ground, so you don't have to change the weight on these frames.

4. On frame 30, move **CtrlLegs** to the left to center the spine over the right foot, and click Set Keys.

5. On frame 40, move **CtrlLegs** slightly to the left, and click **Set Keys**.

6. On frame 60, move **CtrlLegs** to the right to balance the character over its left leg.

You have now created a basic walk cycle.

7. Save the scene as **CharAnimWalkLegs02**.max.

If you like, you can open *CharAnimRig.max* and animate the walk cycle again with the arms swinging opposite the legs.

## TRACK VIEW

Track View is like the Trackbar on steroids. It's a comprehensive chart where you can find information on every key on every object. With Track View, you can change the animation's timing, loop the animation, change the interpolation between keys, and much more.

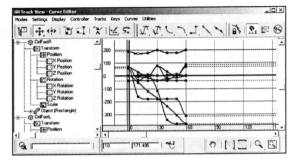

Track View has two modes (displays), the Dope Sheet and the Curve Editor. The Dope Sheet displays all keys as dots, while the Curve Editor shows curves between keys so you can see the interpolation. Each has its own uses.

The Curve Editor shows you each animation track as a set of curves connecting the keys, with the curves representing the interpolation between the keys. You can't really tell what the animation looks like by looking at a curve, but you can spot problem areas by looking for spikes or other odd shapes in the curve. You can also change the default interpolation between keys, which will change the shape of the curve.

The Curve Editor is also where you loop animation. When you loop a sequence of keys, the curves for the looped keys also appear in the Curve Editor. This makes it easy to how the animation flows throughout the active time segment.

The Dope Sheet shows each key on each track as a separate dot. You can click a key to find out its value, and change it right on the Track View window.

To access the Track View graphs, choose *Graph Editors menu > Track View - Dope Sheet* or *Track View > Curve Editor.*

 You can also access a miniature version of the Curve Editor by clicking the Mini Curve Editor (Toggle) button at the left end of the Trackbar.

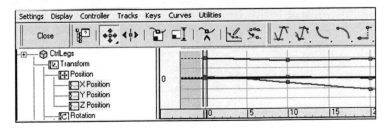

In this tutorial, you will loop a simple walk cycle using the Curve Editor.

### Prepare the Scene

1. Load *CharAnimLoop01.max* from the *Animation/Scenes* folder on the CD.

2. Play the animation.

   This is a version of the walk cycle you created in the last tutorial. You are going to loop this walk cycle using Track View, then use Track View again to spot and solve problems with the looping animation.

   To see the looped animation, you'll need more frames.

3. Click **Time Configuration**, and set **Length** to 300.

### Loop the Frames

1. Select all the control objects.

2. Choose *Graph Editors menu > Track View - Curve Editor*.

   In the Curve Editor, you can see a series of curves. All the curves for all the selected objects are shown at the same time. When you work with the curves later, you will work with them one at a time.

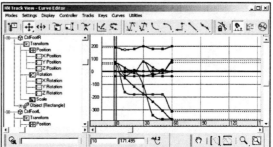

3. On the Track View toolbar, click **Parameter Curve Out-of-Range Types**.

   The Parameter Curve Out-of-Range Types dialog appears.

   An *out-of-range parameter curve* is a curve outside the range of the currently set keys. In this animation, keys have been set on frames 0 through 60. You use this dialog to specify what the animation should do when it goes beyond the currently set keys.

   By default, the out-of-range parameter curve is set to **Constant**. This means the animation stays the same after it reaches frame 60. You can see these curves in the curve editor, where each curve turns into a straight, dotted line after frame 60.

4. On the Parameter Curve Out-of-Range Types dialog, click the right arrow under **Relative Repeat**.

Relative Repeat is a type of looping where the animation repeats relative to the last keyframe. If you had selected **Loop** instead, the character would keep going back to its original location and starting all over again.

5. Click **OK** to close the Parameter Curve Out-of-Range Types dialog. but leave Track View open for now.

6. Play the animation.

The character walks and walks and walks.

### Fix a Looping Curve

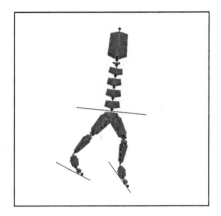

If you study the looped animation closely from frames 250-300, you will find that the animation has some problems that become apparent around this time. The right foot becomes more and more tilted as the animation goes on, the legs become much straighter, and the hips lean to one side.

These problems are an indication that the keys on one or more objects don't match on the first and last frames. Any slight offset is compounded each time the animation loops, so the problem becomes obvious only after it has looped several times.

In particular, the tilted right foot indicates that the rotation of **CtrlFootR** doesn't match on the first and last keyframes. The straightening legs and leaning hips tell you there's a problem with **CtrlLegs**, where its X and Z axis values don't match on the first and last keyframes.

You will fix these problems with Track View, starting with **CtrlLegs**.

1. In the Curve Editor, scroll through the listings at the left find the animation tracks for **CtrlLegs**.

2. Under **Position**, click **X Position**.

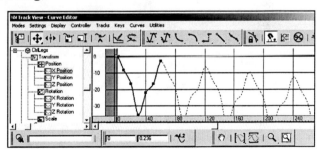

Now you can see just the curve for this track. In the display area of the Curve Editor, you can clearly see that the curve for the X position gradually sinks down. This is an indication that the first and last keyframes don't match.

3. Click the first key dot on the curve.

At the bottom of the Curve Editor are two entry areas. One shows the keyframe number, which is 0. The other shows the value of the key. In this case, the value is 0.236.

4. Click the last key on the curve, at frame 60.

5. In the entry area, enter **0.236**, and press **[Enter]**.

The curve now shows the animation looping perfectly, with the curve following the same pattern at all times without gradually going higher or lower.

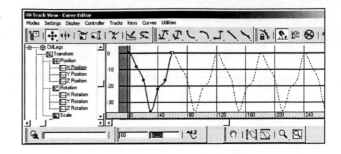

## Fix the Remaining Curves

1. Highlight the **Z Position** listing for **CtrlLegs**.

The curve for the Z value gradually rises.

2. Click the dot on the curve at frame 0 to get the value of the key, then click on the dot at frame 60 and enter the value.

3. Locate the **X Rotation** track for **CtrlFootR**, and use the same technique to fix the curve.

4. Play the animation. It now loops perfectly throughout.

5. Save the scene as **CharAnimLoop02.max**.

> ☙ **TIP** ☙
>
> *You can copy a key value from one entry area with [Ctrl-C] and paste it into another with [Ctrl-V]. Be sure to press [Enter] after pasting the value.*

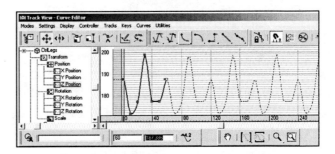

# ANIMATION PRINCIPLES

Once upon a time, there was a little company called Disney. From the 1920's to the 1960's, founder Walt Disney and his crew of animators practically invented the field of animation. The principles they discovered and the terminology they used persist to this day, even in the field of computer-generated animation.

Here, we'll look at the principles of animation developed at Disney Studios, which are still in constant use by the best character animators today. Then we'll explore ways to implement these rules in 3ds max.

"But," you say, "they were drawing each frame by hand. I'm using a computer. Surely the rules are different!" Not true. The way we put the rules into practice has changed; computers have taken over a lot of the repetitive tasks. However, to make an animation that an audience will want to watch, you'll need to know these important rules, and how to use them in your own work.

- *Exaggeration.* Truly entertaining animation doesn't just mimic real life, it exaggerates it. Whatever the character is doing, show it large.

- *Timing.* This refers to the amount of time an action takes. In general, some of your actions will have to be timed like real-life motions so the audience knows what's going on. For actions that are fast or slow in real life, exaggerate the timing. This means fast actions should be very fast, and slow actions should be slower.

**TIP**

To calculate timing, you will need to know the frame rate of your final animation. For example, if an action should take half a second and you're animating at 30 frames per second (fps), then the action should be 15 frames long.

- *Squash and Stretch.* Animated characters can be bent, stretched and squashed into all kinds of positions. Use squash and stretch to exaggerate motion, to make the character double over into a curled position, or stretch its torso, arms and legs into athletic leaps.

- *Anticipation and Follow-through.* Before the character takes action, show an anticipatory motion just before so the audience knows something's about to happen. After the action, show the results of the action.

- *Overlapping Action.* The character should always be doing at least two things at once. For example, if he's waving his arms, he could stand on tiptoe to get attention, or look around wildly for help.

- *Secondary Motion.* If the character is wearing a hat or some loose clothing, or has a long appendage such as a tail, these should be animated separately to respond to the character's motion.

- *Arcs.* Move body parts in arcs, not straight lines.

- *Staging.* Avoid having both sides of the character's body posed identically, and keep the character moving at all times.

These principles should be used in all your character animation, regardless of the tools you use to create it.

## LEARNING TO USE THE PRINCIPLES

One of the best ways to study how these principles are used in practice is to look at as many professional productions as possible. To improve your own abilities to use these principles, you can:

- Watch animated films and television shows with the sound turned off. This works equally well with traditionally-animated and 3D-animated shows and movies. How many of the principles can you spot?

- Go to websites that feature professional 3D animation. Animators seeking work frequently post their *demo reels* (work samples) on these websites. The advantage of looking at animation online is that you often have the opportunity to email the artist with questions about his or her work.

- Show your work-in-progress to others. The animation process has been collaborative since its earliest days, and even seasoned veterans will ask another animator for an opinion or idea. When it comes to helping beginners, I'm constantly surprised by how willing the pros are to offer constructive critiques. Of course, you shouldn't make a pest of yourself; work for the best quality you can before seeking a critique.

In the next tutorial, you will explore how to use the animation principles in practice with 3ds max.

## Tutorial A4: Animating an Action Sequence

In this exercise, you'll load a simple animation that contains just a few keyframes, and use the principles of animation to improve it.

### Load the Scene

1. Load *CharAnimCatch01.max* from the *Animation/Scenes* folder on the CD.

   This scene contains a brief animation of a character being hit by a ball. Not very good, is it?

2. Look at the list of animation principles and see if you can spot what's missing.

   Is the timing good? How could it be improved? Is there any anticipation or follow-through?

### Adjust the Action Timing

You can easily tighten up the timing of the hit from the ball by moving the keys on the Trackbar.

1. Select all the objects in the scene, including the ball, and look at the Trackbar.

2. Move the keys closer together so they are only two or three frames apart.

3. Move all the keys so the first one occurs around frame 60.

4. Play the animation.

   The action is better, but the sequence still needs work.

### Add Anticipation

The character isn't doing anything before he gets hit by the ball. Let's give it some anticipatory motions. To rough out the motion, you'll use the Set Key system.

1. At the bottom right of the screen, select the *Control Objects* selection set.

2. Click **Key Filters**, and turn on **Position**, **Rotation**, and **Custom Attributes**. Turn off all other options, and close the dialog.

3. Turn on **Set Key**.

4. On frame 0, give the character the pose of a person preparing to catch a ball. Exaggerate the pose as much as you like. Click **Set Keys**.

   Don't forget to pose the clavicles and spine.

5. On frame 10 or 15, put the character in a different pose. You can lean the spine in a different direction, or move **CtrlLegs** to shift the character's weight. Click **Set Keys** to set the pose.

6. Set up four or five more poses, until the last pose you set is 10-15 frames away from the character's pose when it gets hit by the ball.

7. Turn off **Set Key**.

**Remove the Twins**

In the animation industry, a character that's posed identically on both sides is referred to as *twins*. Twins are considered bad form in character animation because they're boring. If a pose is boring, it shouldn't be part of your animation!

On the frame where the character gets hit by the ball, it has a twins pose. You can fix this easily by varying the character in some way.

1. Turn on **Auto Key**.

2. On the frame where the character gets hit by the ball, vary the pose by moving **CtrlLegs** to shift its weight, by tilting the spine, or by moving one or both of its hands.

**Add Follow-Through**

The animation now has anticipation and better staging. Now, we'll add some follow-through motions.

When the character hits the ground, it just lies there. Let's add some overlapping motion to make the follow-through more interesting.

1. On the frame where the character hits the ground, move its feet up a bit in the Left viewport.

2. Go to a frame 3-4 frames later. In the Left viewport, move **CtrlLegs** up a bit.

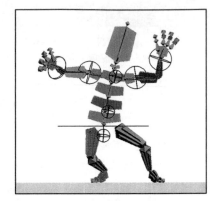

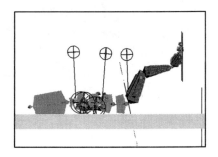

3. A few frames later, move **CtrlLegs** back down.

4. Play the animation.

   Now the character anticipates the hit, and bounces a little when it lands.

5. Work with the timing of the motions until you are satisfied with the animation.

   If you like, you can unhide the mesh and render the animation.

6. Save the scene as **CharAnimCatch02.max**.

   This tutorial gives you an idea of how you can implement the principles of animation when working with 3ds max. In practice, you would work with the timing and motions a great deal before pronouncing the animation finished.

   To see two other versions of this animation, load the files *CharAnimCatch02.max* and *CharAnimCatch03.max* from the CD.

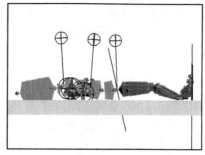

# MODIFIERS AND CONTROLLERS

3ds max has several modifiers and controllers that you can use to implement the principles of animation.

## MODIFIERS

Modifiers are designed to be applied to mesh objects. Usually (but not always), you'll apply these modifiers to non-skinned objects. These would include the head, and any ancillary objects such as a hat or antennae.

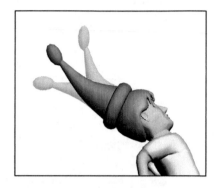

- *Flex modifier.* This modifier adds secondary motion by making the model respond automatically to movement. You can use it to make a hat or antennae bounce around, or to make a big belly jiggle.

- *Linked XForm modifier.* You can use this modifier to link specific vertices or other sub-objects to another object. If you animate the parent objects, the sub-objects will also animate.

☃ **TIP** ☃

*Linked xform means "linked transform."*

- *Squeeze and Stretch modifiers.* These modifiers make objects deform by squashing and stretching.

- *Morpher modifier.* You can use the Morpher modifier to *morph* (gradually change) between different mesh objects with the same number of vertices. This technique is particularly useful for animating facial expressions and speech. You will learn more about this modifier later in this chapter.

 Rather than use modifiers, you might be tempted use the Scale transforms on the Main Toolbar to animate objects squashing and stretching. However, this will create problems in your animation. The Scale transforms don't work well with linked objects, so you should avoid using them in character animation.

## CONTROLLERS

Controllers (also known as *constraints*) can also be used to animate the character.

- *Noise Controller.* This controller can give an object random movement.

- *Link Constraint.* You can use the Link Constraint to cause an object to be linked to different objects on different frames.

In the next tutorial, you will use a link constraint and Linked XForm modifier to animate a scene.

---

## Tutorial A5: Animating with Modifiers and Controllers

### Load the Scene

1. Load the file *CharAnimLanding01.max* from the *Animation/Scenes* folder on the CD.

   This file contains a plank, a dummy object, and a character rig.

2. Play the animation.

   The character lands on the plank around frame 25. The dummy object moves up and down after the character lands.

### Apply a Linked Xform Modifier

The dummy object has been animated to simulate a *stagger* effect. This is a traditional animation effect where an object moves back and forth less and less over a series of frames, then finally comes to rest.

You will use the dummy object and a **Linked Xform** modifier to animate the plank wobbling as the character lands on it.

1. Select the plank, and add a **Mesh Select** modifier to it.

2. At the **Vertex** sub-object level, select the two rows of vertices just above the dummy object.

3. In the Soft Selection rollout, turn on **Use Soft Selection**, and set **Falloff** to about **1250**.

   This will extend the soft selection nearly to the ends of the plank.

4. Without exiting the **Vertex** sub-object level, apply a **Linked XForm** modifier to the plank.

5. Click **Pick Control Object**, and click the dummy object.

6. Play the animation.

   The plank now wobbles when the character lands on it. Its vertices follow the dummy object, with a lesser effect at the ends of the plank according to the soft selection.

### Assign a Link Constraint

After the character lands on the plank, its body should move up and down to match the motion of the plank. You can create this effect by linking the body control to the dummy object.

You really only want the body to follow the dummy object after it lands. You can use a link constraint to cause the body control to link to the dummy object only at a specific frame.

1. Go to frame 30.

2. Select **CtrlBody**.

3. Choose *Animation menu > Constraints > Link Constraints*, and click the dummy object.

On the **Motion** panel, you can see the Link Params rollout. It shows you that the link to the dummy object **Dummy Bounce** begins on frame 30.

4. Play the animation.

Now the character follows the motion of the plank as the plank bends.

5. Save the scene as **CharAnimLanding02.max**.

### Animate Squash and Stretch

Now you must animate the character squashing and stretching after the landing. You will not squash or stretch the body mesh, but will use exaggerated poses to suggest squashing and stretching.

1. Set the **Selection Filter** to *Shapes*.

2. Turn on **Auto Key**.

3. On frame 30, select all the control objects. Right-click the time slider, and set a **Position** and **Rotation** key for all selected objects at this frame.

4. On frame 38, move and rotate the control objects to pose the character in a curled position.

This will simulate an exaggerated pose after a hard landing.

**☀ TIP ☀**

*The Selection Filter is at the left side of the Main Toolbar. By default, it is set to "All".*

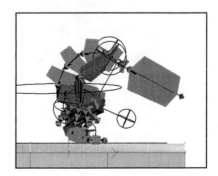

5. On frame 44, straighten up the character and make him arch back a little.

6. On frame 48, curl him over a little.

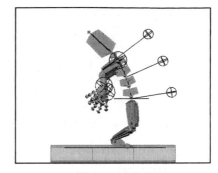

7. Pose the character a few more times, alternating between curling and arching the character every few frames. You can also scrub to intermediate frames and make any corrections necessary.

8. After the character comes to rest, have him look around to the right and left. Be sure to animate the character's head turning in an arc, where the neck and head swing forward slightly as he turns.

To quickly jump from keyframe to keyframe, you can turn on the **Key Mode Toggle** at the bottom right of the screen. This causes the **Previous Frame** and **Next Frame** buttons to become the **Previous Key** and **Next Key** buttons. You can use these buttons to jump from one key to the next for the selected object.

## Add the Flex Modifier

1. Unhide the object **Hat**.

This hat is currently linked to **BoneHead**. It animates with the character, but it's very stiff. You'll use the **Flex** modifier to make it flop around in response to the motion.

2. Select the hat, and go to the **Vertex** sub-object level.

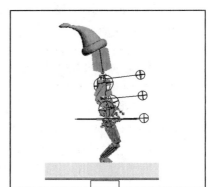

3. At frame 0, zoom in on the hat in the Left viewport, and select the vertices that make up the pom-pom at the top of the hat.

4. Turn on **Use Soft Selection**, and increase the **Falloff** value until it reaches about 3/4 of the way down the hat.

5. While still at the **Vertex** sub-object level, apply the **Flex** modifier to the hat.

6. Scrub the time slider to see the result.

If the hat flops around too much, try decreasing the **Flex** value on the Parameters rollout to a lower value such as **0.1** or **0.3**.

7. Save the scene as **CharAnimLanding03.max**.

You can find a finished version of this scene in the file *CharAnimLanding04.max*, and in the rendered animation *CharAnimLanding04.avi* in the *Animation/AVI* folder on the CD. This file has motion blur applied to the character mesh and the plank to make the motion look smoother.

# FACIAL ANIMATION

Although you can go a long way toward animating a complete scene simply by animating the character's body, you can add greatly to the expressiveness of the sequence by animating the character's face.

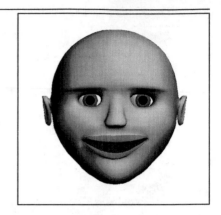

At the very least, you will want the character to blink its eyes. You can also animate the character reacting to its circumstances with various facial expressions, and animate its mouth to make it speak in sync with a soundtrack.

With facial animation, there are three types of animation to consider:

- Animation of the eyes to look in various directions
- Animation of the face for expressions, including blinking
- Mouth animation for speech

## EYE ANIMATION

One of the easiest ways to breathe more life into an animation is to make the eyes look in various directions during the sequence.

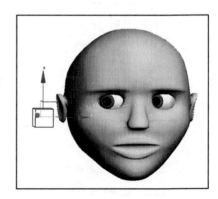

To accomplish this, you can use a *look-at constraint* to force the eyes to always look at a control object somewhere in front of the head. The object they look at is called the *look-at target*. Making the eyes look in different directions then becomes a simple matter of moving the look-at target.

To use this tool, you will need to create separate objects for the eyes. Usually, you will start with spheres, and change their shapes slightly to fit the facial model.

# Tutorial A6: ANIMATING THE EYES

In this tutorial, you will shape the eyeballs to fit the head, and add a look-at constraint so you can animate the eyes looking in different directions.

## Try out a Look-At Constraint

1. Load the file *CharAnimEyes01.max* from the *Animation/Scenes* folder on the CD.

    This scene contains a head similar to the one you created in the *Character Modeling* chapter. The eyes were created as spheres, then converted to Editable Poly objects. The pupils were given different material ID so the pupils and whites can have different colors.

    The scene also contains a dummy object placed a short distance from the head. You will use this object as the look-at target for the eyes.

    In this scene, the eyes were shaped by scaling vertices at the **Vertex** sub-object level. The head has been frozen to prevent you from accidentally selecting it.

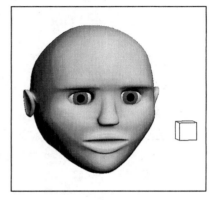

2. Select the right eye.

3. Choose *Animation menu > Constraints > LookAt Constraint*, and click the dummy object in front of the head.

    The eye rolls up into the head. In order for the look-at constraint to work, you must set the appropriate axis for the eye. The eyes were created in the Front viewport, so their local Z axes point straight ahead.

4. In the Motion panel, in the middle of the LookAt Constraint rollout, change the **Select Look-At Axis** to **Z**.

5. For the **aligned to Upnode Axis** option at the bottom of the rollout, choose **Z**.

    This will cause the eye to have the same orientation on its X and Y axes as it had before you added the look-at constraint.

6. Turn off **Viewline Length Absolute**.

    This causes the blue length line to extend all the way to the look-at target.

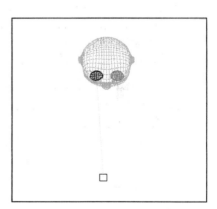

7. Select the left eye, and follow the same steps to set up a look-at constraint for the left eye.

8. In the Top viewport, move the dummy object to the left or right.

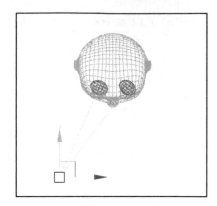

When you move the dummy object way over to the left or right, you can see the eyes rotate in the Top viewport.

There is a slight problem with the eyes. If you watch the User viewport, you can see the edges of the eyes rotating into or out of the eye sockets at the extremes.

To prevent this from occurring, you'll shape the eyes with a different tool: the FFD space warp.

## Create FFD Space Warps

To solve the problem with the eyes, you can use a *free form deformation (FFD)* tool. This tool creates a lattice around an object. You can move the points on the lattice to deform the object. Then, when you use a look-at constraint, the eyes will stay deformed according to the lattice as they rotate to face the look-at target.

There are several FFD tools in 3ds max. For the eyes, you will use a FFD *space warp*. A space warp is similar to a modifier, but it warps the object using a separate gizmo which can stay put while the object moves or rotates. This means the space warp always applies the same deformation to the object regardless of whether the object is animated.

The FFD space warp will keep the eye conformed to the head while the eye rotates to face the look-at target.

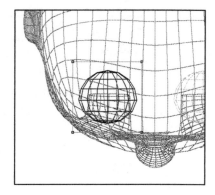

1. Load the file *CharAnimEyesFFD01.max*.

   This file contains the same setup, but the eyes haven't been shaped to fit the head.

2. On the **Create** panel, click **Space Warps**. Choose *Geometric/Deformable* from the dropdown menu, and click **FFD (Box)**.

3. Click **Set Number of Points**, and set **Length**, **Width** and **Height** to **2**.

4. In the Top viewport, click and drag to create a space warp around the right eye. Drag again to set the space warp's height, and click to finish creating it.

The space warp is shaped like a box, with a control point at each corner of the box. You will use this box to warp the eye in a later step.

5. Use **Align** to align the space warp with the right eye.

6. On the **Modify** panel, name the space warp **SWEyeR**.

7. Set the space warp's **Length**, **Width** and **Height** to **24**.

   This will make the space warp sufficiently large to encompass the eye.

8. In the Deform group, choose the **All Vertices** option.

   This will cause the space warp to deform all vertices in the eye, even if they aren't inside the space warp. If the space warp completely encompasses the eye, this won't be an issue. However, setting this option prevents this problem from occurring even if the space warp is a little too small for the eye.

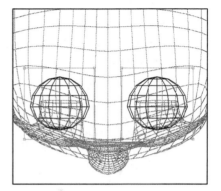

9. Make a copy of the space warp, and name it **SWEyeL**. Align this space warp with the left eye.

**Bind the Eyes to the Space Warps**

In order for a space warp to affect an object, you must bind the object to it.

1. Select the right eye. Make sure the eye itself is selected, not the space warp.

2. On the Main Toolbar, click **Bind to Space Warp**.

3. Press the **[H]** key on the keyboard, and choose **SWEyeR** from the Select Space Warp dialog.

   A new modifier, **FFD Binding**, appears on the stack for the right eye.

4. Select the left eye, and click **Bind to Space Warp**. Press the **[H]** key and choose **SWEyeL**.

**Warp the Eyes with the Space Warps**

1. Select the space warp on the right eye.

2. On the **Modify** panel, expand the listing to show the **Control Points** sub-object. Highlight **Control Points**.

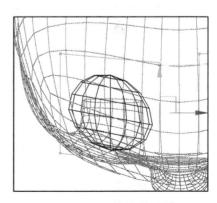

3. In the Top viewport, move the control points to skew the eye and make it follow the shape of the head, as shown in the picture.

As you move the control points, you will see the eye deforming to follow the shape of the lattice. Check your work in the User viewport to make sure the eye looks good.

4. Turn off **Control Points** when you have finished.

5. Select the space warp on the left eye. Use the control points on this space warp to skew the left eye in the direction opposite the right. Turn off **Control Points** when you have finished.

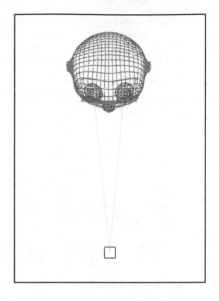

### Set up the Look-At Constraint

Now you're ready to apply the look-at constraint to the eyes.

1. Select the right eye.

2. Choose *Animation menu > Constraints > LookAt Constraint*, and click the dummy object in front of the head.

3. In the Motion panel, set the **Select Look-At Axis** to **Z**, and choose **Z** for the **aligned to Upnode Axis** option. Turn off **Viewline Length Absolute**.

4. Select the left eye, and follow the same steps to set up a look-at constraint on the left eye.

5. Move the dummy object to the left or right.

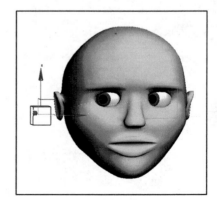

The eyes follow the look-at target, but they stay deformed to the shape of the head as they turn.

6. Save the scene as **CharAnimEyesFFD02.max**.

## FACIAL EXPRESSIONS AND SPEECH

You can animate facial expressions and speech with the Morpher modifier. This modifier works by *morphing* (changing) between different versions of the same object to produce animation.

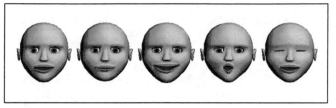

To use the morpher modifier with a character's head, you must first create several copies of the head, and arrange the vertices on each copy into different expressions. The various copies are called *morph targets*. Then you can apply the Morpher modifier to one of the heads, and use it to animate the head to match specific morph targets on different frames.

The Morpher modifier requires all objects to have the same number of vertices. Therefore, you must take the time to set up the first copy of the head with all the vertices you think you will need. For example, if the character will open its mouth, the initial head must have a mouth cavity and sufficient vertices at the lips to form the expressions. If the character is going to blink, you must have polygons that can act as eyelids.

If you want the character to speak, you will need to model a number of mouth positions that represent the major vowel and consonant sounds. These sounds, and the facial positions that represent them, are called *phonemes*. You don't need a phoneme for every letter of the alphabet, because the mouth position is the same for many sounds. For example, your mouth looks nearly the same when you pronounce the letter "B" as it does when you say "P".

In this book, you'll learn to create facial expressions and animate them with the Morpher modifier. We won't be animating speech, but the techniques you'll learn with the Morpher modifier can easily be applied to this type of animation.

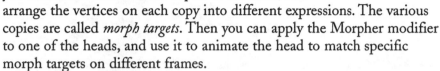

### ☼ TIP ☼

*You can find a list of phonemes and their corresponding facial positions in any comprehensive book on character animation.. The phonemes are the same for both traditional and computer animation.*

# Tutorial A7: Morphing Facial Expressions

In this tutorial, you'll create several versions of a single head, model different facial expressions, and morph between them with the **Morpher** modifier. You can use this technique with any model to animate the character's face.

**Load the Head Scene**

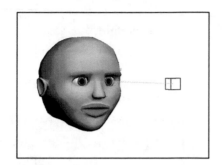

1. Load *CharAnimHead01.max* from the *Animation/Scenes* folder on the CD.

   This scene contains a single head with its mouth and eyes in a neutral pose. The eyes are rigged with FFD space warps to follow the dummy object when it moves.

   The head has **MeshSmooth** applied to it. You'll need to see the results of **MeshSmooth** at certain times while you work, but you'll need to work at the **Editable Poly** level of the object.

   For now, you'll turn off the **Show end result on/off toggle** so you can work with the vertices, but you'll turn it back on as needed so you can see the results of **MeshSmooth**.

2. Select **Head_Base**, the head in the scene.

3. On the **Modify** panel, turn off the **Show end result on/off toggle** if necessary.

**Create a Material for the Mouth Cavity**

The head needs a mouth cavity. This will make the facial expressions look more realistic when the character opens its mouth.

Before extruding these polygons to form the mouth cavity, you'll give them a unique material ID. This will enable you to assign a different material to the inside of the mouth and make it whatever color you like.

1. Open the Material Editor, and select the material called **Head**.

   This multi/sub-object material has two materials, one for the flesh color and the other for the lips. You will add a third color for the inside of the mouth.

2. Click **Set Number**, and set the number of materials to **3**.

3. Change the color of the last material to a dark red color. If you like, you can also change the name of the material to **Mouth Cavity**.

4. Close the Material Editor.

5. Go to the **Polygon** sub-object level for the **Editable Poly**.

6. In the Front viewport, select the two polygons that make up the inside of the mouth.

7. In the Polygon Properties rollout, set **Material ID** to 3.

   When you extrude the selected polygons into the head, the new polygons will also have this material ID and material.

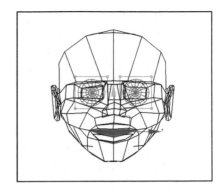

### Extrude the Mouth Cavity

1. While watching the Left viewport, extrude the selected polygons into the character's head.

2. In the Edit Geometry rollout, click **Make Planar**.

   This straightens out the selected polygons, making them all lie in the same plane. This will make it easier to adjust the vertices in the steps that follow.

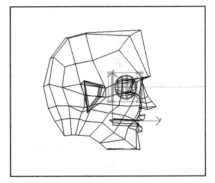

3. Turn on the **Show end result on/off toggle**.

4. Go to the **Vertex** sub-object level for the Editable Poly.

5. Select the vertices at the end of the mouth cavity, and scale the vertices to make the inside of the cavity larger.

   Be sure to check your work in both the Front and Left viewports.

6. When you have finished, turn off the **Show end result on/off toggle** and turn off the **Vertex** sub-object level.

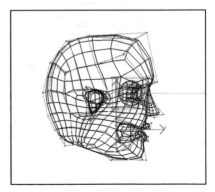

### Create Copies of the Head

The **Morpher** modifier works only with objects with the same number of vertices. The easiest way to create these objects is to make several copies of the base object, and move vertices on each one.

1. In the Front viewport, create four copies of the head to the right of the original.

The head copies won't have any eyes. You will use the **Morpher** modifier without affecting the eyes, so you don't need a set of eyes for each head.

2. Name the copies **Head_CloseMouth, Head_Smile, Head_Ooo,** and **Head_Blink**.

3. In the Top viewport, move each copy forward individually so you can see each one's profile in the Left viewport.

4. Save the scene as **CharAnimHead02.max**.

### Create the First Facial Expression

1. In the Front viewport, zoom in on **Head_CloseMouth**.

2. Go to the **Vertex** sub-object level for the **Editable Poly**.

3. In the Selection rollout, turn on **Ignore Backfacing**.

4. Move vertices around the mouth area to close the mouth in a neutral expression.

5. Check your work in both the Left and Front viewports, and turn on the **Show end result on/off toggle** as necessary to see how the facial expression looks with smoothing.

6. Turn off the **Vertex** sub-object level when you're done so you can select the next head.

### Create the Remaining Facial Expressions

For each facial expression, you should zoom in on the head in the Front viewport, and turn on **Ignore Backfacing** while working at the **Vertex** sub-object level. Check your work in both the Left and Front viewports, and turn **MeshSmooth** on and off as necessary to see the final result will look.

You might also find it useful to work in *Smooth+Highlights* mode with *Edged Faces* turned on. You can also use soft selection when working with sets of vertices to move entire regions of the face.

☀ **TIP** ☀

*If you prefer to have a set of eyes present when you model each facial expression, you can copy the eyes to each head. If you do so, be sure to copy the entire eye setup, including the FFD space warps and the look-at target.*

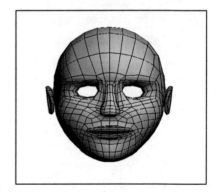

1. For **Head_Smile**, pose the mouth vertices into a smile. When you smile, the corners of your mouth not only move away from the center of your face, but they move slightly toward the back of your head. In addition, your lips flatten out to some degree.

   To make the smiling expression, move not just the vertices at the mouth, but also those on the nose, cheekbones, and eyes just a little bit. You can also move and rotate the vertices at the corners of the eyes to make the smile "reach" the eyes. This will make this expression look more natural during animation.

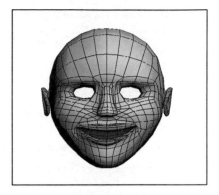

2. For **Head_Ooo**, pose the lips in a pucker, as if the character were saying, "Ooo." Push the bottom of the nose upward a little, and squint the eyes slightly.

3. For **Head_Blink**, move the eyelids close together to close the eyes.

   This can be the trickiest expression to create. There are sets of vertices near the edges of the eyes specifically for closing the eyelids. You will have to carefully select these vertices and move them up or down to close the eyes. Use *Wireframe* display, **Arc Rotate**, or any means you need to find and select these vertices.

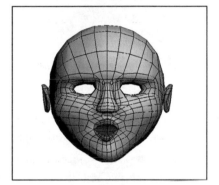

   Be sure to check your work with **MeshSmooth**, as the eyelids won't close as much when **MeshSmooth** is turned on.

   You only have to adjust the eyelid vertices for this expression. When you use this expression with the **Morpher** modifier, you will use only the selection of vertices used to close the eyes. This will allow you to combine this expression with others.

4. On **Head_Blink**, select the vertices you moved to close the eyelids.

5. In the **Named Selection Sets** entry area, enter the name **Eyelids**.

   This creates a selection set that you will be able to access only when you are at the **Vertex** sub-object level. By creating this selection set, you ensure you'll be able to select the vertices again if you lose the selection by accident.

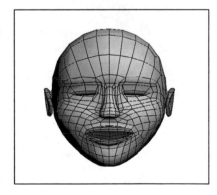

6. Turn off the **Vertex** sub-object level for **Head_Blink**.

7. Save the scene as **CharAnimHead03.max**.

## Apply the Morpher Modifier

1. Hide the space warps and dummy object to make it easier to see **Head_Base**.

   You'll apply the **Morpher** modifier to **Head_Base** below its **MeshSmooth** modifier. The system will respond faster if it's morphing unsmoothed meshes, because they have fewer vertices.

   When you ask the **Morpher** modifier to load morph targets, it will only find those that have the same number of vertices as **Head_Base** before **MeshSmooth** is applied. Therefore, you have to remove **MeshSmooth** from all the other heads before you can use them as morph targets.

2. Remove the **MeshSmooth** modifier from all the heads except **Head_Base**.

3. Select **Head_Base**.

4. Select the Editable Poly level for **Head_Base**, and apply the **Morpher** modifier.

   Make sure the **Morpher** modifier appears below **MeshSmooth** on the stack.

5. In the Channels List rollout, click **Load Multiple Targets**. Select all the heads that appear on the list.

## Morph the Facial Expressions

The Morpher modifier works with *channels*. Each channel holds a different morph target. In the Channel List rollout, each morph target appears in its own channel.

You morph to different targets by animating the channel percentage. When a morph target's percentage is set to 100, the face takes on 100% of that facial expression.

1. Turn on **Auto Key**.

2. Go to frame 20, and set the percentage for **Head_CloseMouth** to 100.

   This morphs the head to match this morph target.

3. Go to frame 25, and set the percentage for **Head_CloseMouth** to 0.

4. On frame 25, set the percentage for **Head_Smile** to 100.

## ☼ TIP ☼

*This is similar to the workflow you used for skinning, where you applied the Skin modifier below MeshSmooth.*

## ☼ TIP ☼

*You can mix morph targets by setting two or more percentages to values less than 100.*

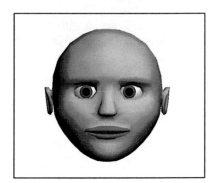

Keys for each percentage are stored separately, so the **Head_Smile** percentage will go from 0 to 100 over frames 0 to 25. To keep the character from smiling until frame 20, you will have to set a key for this channel at frame 20.

5. Go back to frame 20, and change the percentage for **Head_Smile** to **0**.

Now you will animate the eyes blinking around frame 25. You can tell the Morpher modifier to use only the last vertices selected to form the morph target for this channel.

6. Click **Head_Blink** in the Channel List rollout to select that channel. In the Channel Parameters rollout, turn on **Use Vertex Selection**.

7. Go to frame 25, and set the **Head_Blink** percentage to 100.

The eyes close, but the smile expression does not change. This is because the channel is morphing only the selected vertices on the eyelids.

Now you must set the **Head_Blink** percentages to **0** a few frames before and after the blink.

8. On frames 22 and 27, and set the **Head_Blink** percentage to **0**.

This creates a blink with three frames to close the eyes, and two frames to open them.

If you play the animation, you will see the character close its mouth, then smile and blink.

9. Save the scene as **CharAnimHead05.max**.

**Finish the Animation**

Now you will set up the remaining keys in preparation to use this head animation with a body animation sequence you created earlier.

1. Use **Time Configuration** to set the total number of frames to 120.

2. On frame 55, and set **Head_CloseMouth** to 100 and **Head_Smile** to 0.

3. Go back to frame 50, and set **Head_CloseMouth** to 0 to keep the mouth closed until that frame. Set **Head_Smile** to 100.

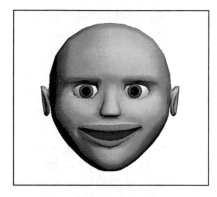

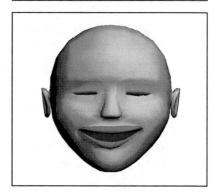

4. Set the remaining keys as follows. They are listed in the order you should set them.

   If you don't want to set all these keys, you can load *CharAnimHead06.max* from the *Animation/Scenes* folder on the CD to see the final sequence.

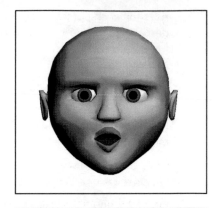

| Frame | Expression | Percentage |
|-------|------------|------------|
| 50 | Head_Blink | 100 |
| 47 | Head_Blink | 0 |
| 52 | Head_Blink | 0 |
| 85 | Head_CloseMouth | 0 |
| 85 | Head_Ooo | 100 |
| 80 | Head_CloseMouth | 100 |
| 80 | Head_Ooo | 0 |
| 80 | Head_Blink | 100 |
| 77 | Head_Blink | 0 |
| 82 | Head_Blink | 0 |
| 102 | Head_CloseMouth | 100 |
| 102 | Head_Ooo | 0 |
| 102 | Head_Blink | 100 |
| 100 | Head_CloseMouth | 0 |
| 100 | Head_Ooo | 100 |
| 100 | Head_Blink | 0 |

> ☀ **TIP** ☀
>
> *Any time the facial expression changes is a good time for a blink.*

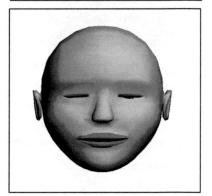

The animation should end with the character's eyes and mouth closed. If you like, you can play the animation to see what it looks like.

5. If you removed the **MeshSmooth** modifier from **Head_Base**, turn it back on now.

6. Save the scene as **CharAnimHead06.max**.

### Prepare the Head for Merging

Now you can merge the heads into a scene with an existing character rig, and use the facial expressions in conjunction with body animation.

1. Hide all the heads except **Head_Base**.

2. Unhide the space warps and dummy object.

To prepare the head for use in a scene, you will link all the objects to a single object. Then you only have to link that one object to the character rig's head bone.

3. Create a dummy object about half the size of the head. Name the dummy object **DummyHeadAll**.

4. Move the dummy object so it sits just on top of the head.

 5. Select all the objects in the scene except **DummyHeadAll** (the head, eyes, space warps, and look-at dummy), and link them to **DummyHeadAll**.

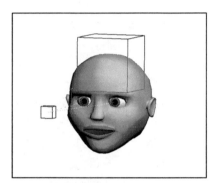

6. Test the linkage by moving **DummyHeadAll**. The head, eyes, space warps, and look-at dummy should move along with it.

7. Save the scene as **CharAnimHead07.max**.

### Merge the Head into the Action Scene

1. Load the scene *CharAnimCatch03.max*, either your own version or the one from the *Animation/Scenes* folder on the CD.

2. Play the animation.

This is a version of the scene you animated earlier, with the character waving his arms, getting hit by a ball, and falling down.

3. Unhide **Skater_Mesh_Head**, and delete it.

This is the existing head in the scene. You will be replacing this head with your morphed head, so you can get rid of it.

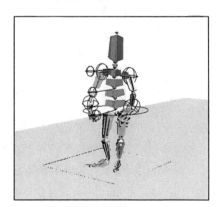

4. Choose *File menu > Merge*, and choose *CharAnimHead07.max*. Select all the objects in the scene, including the morph targets.

Because you hid the morph targets before saving the scene, they come into the current scene already hidden.

### Place the Head

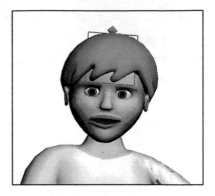

1. Unhide the body and hair mesh objects.

2. On frame 0, move **DummyHeadAll** so the head sits on the head bone, **BoneHead**. If necessary, rotate it to match the rotation of **BoneHead**.

3. Unfreeze all the objects in the scene.

4. Link **DummyHeadAll** to **BoneHead**.

5. Link the hair mesh to **BoneHead**.

6. Hide all the bones and control objects.

7. If the neck protrudes into the mouth cavity, go to the **Vertex** sub-object level of the body mesh's **Editable Poly**, and move the topmost neck vertices down to make the neck nub shorter.

   You can also improve the scene by changing the character's facial or body skin colors so they match.

8. Play or render the animation.

   To see a rendered version of this animation, view the file *CharAnimCatch05.avi* from the *Animation/AVI* folder on the CD.

   The character smiles, blinks, and says "Ooo!" when he's about to catch the ball. When the ball hits him, he closes his eyes, and they remain closed for the duration of the animation.

   To get the facial timing for this animation, I looked for times when the character made a strong move, and changed his facial expression at those times. The blinks also coincide with strong motions.

   If you like, you can also animate the look-at dummy to make the character look in different directions over the course of the action.

9. Save the scene as **CharAnimCatch04.max**.

   You can find a version of this scene that includes lights and materials in the file *CharAnimCatch05.max*.

> ### ☼ TIP ☼
> *To make colors match, you can drag a face or body color to the Color Clipboard utility to hold it. Then you can then select the other material and drag the color from the Color Clipboard to the material.*

# RESOURCES

Congratulations on making your way through this book. You now have the basics of modeling, rigging, and animating characters with 3ds max. I hope you're inspired to experiment and learn more!

There are many resources you can use to further your abilities, whether you prefer books, DVDs, or surfing the Internet.

## BOOKS

### Computer Animation

*Mastering the Art of Production with 3ds max 4*, Michele Bousquet and Jason Busby

*Modeling a Character with 3ds max.* Paul Steed

*Digital Character Animation*, George Maestri

*Character Animation*, Doug Kelly

### Traditional Character Design and Animation Principles

*The Animator's Workbook*, Tony White

*How to Draw Cartoon Characters*, Preston Blair

*Timing in Animation*, Harold Whitaker and John Halas

*Acting for Animators*, Ed Hooks

*Animation from Script to Screen*, Shamus Culhane

*Disney Animation: The Illlusion of Life*, Frank Thomas and Ollie Johnston

*The Human Figure in Motion* and *Animals in Motion*, Edweard Muybridge

## DVDS

These DVDs are available from Maxhelp.com and Discreet.com. They provide a visual approach to learning about character modeling and animation with 3ds max.

*Discreet Advanced Character Modeling DVD*

*Discreet Character Rigging DVD*

*Discreet Advanced Character Animation DVD*

## WEBSITES

For additional assistance, visit these resources on the Internet:

| | |
|---|---|
| Discreet Support Forum | http://support.discreet.com |
| Maxhelp | http://www.maxhelp.com |
| CG Character | http://www.cg-char.com |
| 3D Buzz | http://www.3dbuzz.com |
| CG Training | http://www.cgtraining.com |
| 3D Luvr | http://www.3dluvr.com |
| 3D Cafe | http://www.3dcafe.com |

# INDEX

local axes, coordinates 58
    aligning with another object 105
    determining 120
    relationship to pivot point 101
    relationship to wiring 104
Lock Zoom/Pan 5
LookAt constraint 204, 205-209
low-poly, definition
material
    body 36-37
    eyes 49-50
    face 49-50
    Gradient Ramp map 49-50
    ID 37
    Multi/Sub-Object 36, 49-50
merge
    facial expressions 217-218
    head 53
MeshSmooth modifier
    with Morpher modifier 214
MeshSmooth modifier
    for modeling 19
    Isoline Display 19
    with the Skin modifier 155, 176
Mini Curve Editor 191
mirror
    arm rig 137-138
    leg bones 71
    object 27-28
    Symmetry modifier 35
model
    definition 3
    reference 4
modeling
    arms 13-14, 21
    collar 32-34
    face 42-54
    hair 51-52
    hands 24-29

head 38-54
legs 15, 23
morph targets 212-213
mouth cavity 210-211
shoes, socks 29
sleeves 22
modifier stack 8
modifiers
    FFD Binding 207
    Flex 200, 203
    instanced 155
    Linked XForm 200
    Mesh Select 201
    MeshSmooth 19, 214
    Morpher 200
    remove 67
    Skin 145
    Spherify 39
    Squeeze 200
    Stretch 200
    Symmetry 34, 35
    turn off 19
    UVW map 50
Morpher modifier 200, 209-218
    animating morph targets 214-216
    channels 214
morphing 209
Multi/Sub-Object material 36-37, 49-50
names of character bones 70, 71, 74, 75
Noise Controller 200
nub bones
    not used with Skin modifier 158
orientation constraint 118
overlapping action 196
parameter curve out-of-range types 192
parameter wiring
    methods 86, 98
    using expressions in 90
parent 60